はじめに

ホテルの小さな客室の内装を手掛けたことからトラフの活動が始まりました。私たちの仕事は、指輪などのプロダクトから、インテリア、舞台美術、建築まで幅広い範囲に及んでいます。どんなことであれ、目の前にあることに興味をもって積極的に取り組むことで、さまざまな領域を横断しながら活動してきました。

本書を『インサイド・アウト (Inside Out = 裏返し)』としたのは、トラフの頭の中をさらけ出し、都市＞建築＞インテリア＞家具＞モノ といったヒエラルキーに捉われない、私たちのアプローチをタイトルに込めたからです。

モノ、時間、家具、敷地、素材、都市、といった、建築的なキーワードを手掛かりに、新作を含めたこれまでの作品を再編集することで、それぞれを等価に扱うトラフの取り組みを多角的に感じ取ってもらえたらと思います。

鈴野浩一、禿 真哉

モノから風景をつくる

アジアの街で見掛ける、バルコニーを埋め尽くす植物や洗濯物、商品だらけのマーケットや蚤の市などにいつも魅力を感じる。それは、個人の営みや、使われているモノが外側にあふれて、活気ある街並みをつくり出し、モノが街をつくっている、と言えるからかもしれない。都市計画があり、建築をつくって、内装を施し、最後に家具やモノを置くといった手順ではなく、小さなモノから逆に発想したい。住宅を設計する時に、モノの整理から始めるのは、モノが入ることで息づくような空間を目指しているからで、店舗の計画では、陳列される商品を単なるディスプレイとしてではなく、空間構成の一部として考える。モノや人を含めた総体としての、生き生きとした風景のようなものをつくりたいと思っている。

時間を取り込む

時間とは、出来事や変化を認識するための、時刻というある1点とある1点との間を示す。この、時間という連続性をもつ概念を、設計に取り入れたいと思っている。建築は動かないからこそ、陽の光や雲、星など、自然環境の動きを相対的に感じることができる。1日単位で感じる動きもあれば、季節など1年という単位で感じるものもある。住宅が、そこで営まれ

る人生の、何十年という時間単位の動きを受け止めるように、インテリアやプロダクトにも、その長い時間軸を取り込みたい。プロダクトの経年変化を使う人に委ねるようにすれば、その人ごとの個性を与えることもできる。リノベーションのプロジェクトでは、既存の建物がもつ時間の流れを新しい計画の中に取り込み、両者を一体的に扱いたい。「時間を取り込む」思考によって、モノ、人、空間が継続的な関係性をもてるのではないだろうか。

見えないものを可視化する

太陽の光が大気中の水蒸気に反射することで見える虹や、らせん状に木の葉が舞い上がるつむじ風のように、普段は見えないものが何かをきっかけにして形をもつ現象に、好奇心を抱き続けている。室内に外部環境を取り込む窓のように、意識しないと気付きにくいその場所の環境や地形が、建築を介することであらわになることがある。そこに何かを置く、または仕掛けを与えることで表出する、事物や現象を捉えたいと思っている。それは、光を取り出したり、色の知覚の仕方を気付かせたり、無形のものに形を与えることなのかもしれない。見えるものと見えないものは表裏一体で、互いが干渉することで顕在化するのだと思う。「見えないものを可視化する」ことで、普段何気なく見ている風景の中に、新しい気付きを与えたい。

家具のような建築、建築のような家具

家具と建築の境界線はあるのだろうか。普段、形や空間のスタディは、模型をベースに行っている。模型をひっくり返したり、部分的に壊したり、直感的な試みも容易に行える。また、同じ空間でも、敷地全体を見る1000分の1や、詳細を検討する1分の1など、さまざまな縮尺を使い分ける。引いて見たり、近付いて見たりと視点の移動を繰り返すうち、どこからが家具でどこからが建築なのかを考えさせられてしまう。むしろ、それぞれが専門領域として分かれてしまっていることで、可能性を狭めてしまってはいないか。そんな視点から、家具を設計する時は建築を設計するように、建築を設計する時は家具を設計するように、双方向からのアプローチを試みている。人の居場所をつくるような家具や、人の行動に寄り添った建築など、家具は空間化され、建築は身体に近付いていくように、人と家具と建築の関係を変えていきたいと思っている。

余白をつくる

建築でもプロダクトでも、訪れた人や使う人が関われるような「余白をつくる」ことを意識している。人が能動的に参加できるきっかけや、それぞれがカスタマイズできる自由度、誰もが共有しやすいストーリーがあること、選択的に情報を得られ

る柔軟さがあることなど、「余白をつくる」ことで、人と人、人と空間やプロダクトとの間に、双方向のコミュニケーションを促すことができる。受動的に物事を受け止めるだけでは気付き得ない発見や、つくり手の思惑や想像を超えた、発展的な使い方を生み出せるかもしれない。人が関わることで初めて完成するような、余白をもつ場をつくり出したいと思っている。

敷地を与える

敷地には、そこに建つ建築に作用する強い固有性が備わっている。建築の設計は、敷地の分析や考察から始まる。一方でプロダクトや家具は、使う人や場所が特定されないという自由さがあり、かえって条件がないことにとまどいを感じていた。そこで、持ち運びができるプロダクトにも、使われる場所や状況を敷地に見立て、自ら条件を与えることで、それが置かれる状況をデザインに取り込めるのではないかと考えた。また、ショップなら什器を、住宅なら家具を、敷地と建築の関係性と同じようにつくることで、おのずとそれが特徴や個性となる。建築とその環境、あるいはプロダクトとその空間を、「敷地を与える」ことによって、より一体的なものとして捉えている。

素材から発想する

建築現場や工場で見掛ける、建材や家具の骨組みなどに魅力を感じる。それは、ものが形づくられる前の素材そのものや、家具として仕上がる前の地肌がもつ力強さだけでなく、加工次第で大きく変わる発展性に期待するからだと思う。素材には、見たままのテクスチャーに加え、触れた時の質感や、重さ、硬さなどの物性がある。素材を表面的に扱うだけではなく、テクスチャーや物性、イメージなどを含めて検討することで、素材に対する潜在的なイメージを越えた、新たなアプローチを見付けることができる。また、視野を拡げれば、空気や水など無形のものも、素材として扱うことができるかもしれない。手元にある食材から料理を決めるような感覚で、「素材から発想する」ことの可能性を探っている。

トラフの小さな都市計画

街路に置かれる家具ひとつで都市を変えることはできないだろうか。都市計画というと、土地の区画や用途を決めたり、それらを結ぶインフラを計画したり、大がかりなものを想像してしまう。「小さな都市計画」とは、スケールをぐっと下げて、モノや家具、身近なコミュニティから発想し、都市を捉え直すことだと思っている。それらの小さな試みの積み重ねによって、

人びとが都市にもっと愛着をもてるような仕掛けをつくりたい。建築に興味をもてば、街中が建築のミュージアムのように見え、植物図鑑を片手に散歩に出れば、街中が植物園のようにも見えてくる。例えば公園にシェアできるキッチンがあれば、公園自体がダイニングのように感じられ、街を共有している感覚になる。すでにある街との関わり方を更新することで、都市をもっと豊かな生活の場に変えていきたい。意識や視点を変えて、街との接点をつくり、身の周りの環境から逆に都市を提案する「小さな都市計画」が、都市そのものを変える大きな力になると思っている。

Introduction

TORAFU first became active after working on the interior design of a small hotel guest room. Our work has since been wide-ranging, from products such as rings, to interiors, stage designs, and architecture. We have been active across a diverse range of fields by taking an interest in, and working constructively on, every type of project put before us.

"Inside Out", the title of this book, reveals the thought process behind TORAFU. It also embodies our desire not be fixated on the hierarchy of Cities > Architecture > Interiors > Furniture > Objects.

Using architectural keywords like objects, time, furniture, site, materials and cities as a hint, we hope that people can perceive TORAFU's multifaceted efforts to treat everything equivalently by revisiting all of our work, including our newest endeavors.

Koichi Suzuno, Shinya Kamuro

CREATING SCENERY FROM OBJECTS

We are fascinated by the sight of Asian cities with plants and laundry that fill balconies, and the markets and flea markets overflowing with goods. The way in which an individual's business and possessions spill outside helps to create a lively cityscape; you might even say that these objects are what creates the city. We prefer to start conceptualizing from small objects rather than adhering to the process of urban planning, creating architecture, then interior design followed by the placement of furniture and objects. When designing a residential building, the reason that we start with the arrangement of objects is because we aim for a breathable space in which the objects can fit, not simply to display products like an exhibition, but rather as a part of what composes the space according to the store plans. We hope to create lively scenery as a whole, which includes objects and people.

CAPTURING TIME

Time indicates the interval between two moments in order to perceive events and changes. We would like to incorporate the concept of continuity in time into our designs. Since architecture does not change, you can feel the relative changes in the natural environment, such as sunlight and clouds. In some instances, you can feel the changes day by day while in other instances, you can feel changes each year through the seasons. Just as a residential building is used as a place to support a life over several decades, we also want to introduce a long timeline into our interior designs and products. If we entrust it to people that will make use of products as they change over the years, they will each be able to confer personality on each other. For renovation projects, we want to incorporate the passage of time of an existing building into our new plans and treat these two things in a unified manner. The continuous relationship between objects, people, and space can surely be maintained through this idea of *capturing time*.

VISUALIZING THE INVISIBLE

We are continually interested in the phenomenon of something unseen being triggered into taking on a shape; similar to rainbows that become visible when sunlight reflects off of water droplets in the atmosphere or the leaves that fly up into a spiral shape during a whirlwind. Like a window that incorporates the external environment inside a room, architecture acts as an intermediary to expose a location's environment and terrain that would otherwise be hard to notice if you were not conscious of it. We strive to capture things and phenomena that are expressed by placing something or arranging something in a certain place. Perhaps this involves giving form to formless things, as in producing light or forcing an awareness of a method of color perception. We believe that visible and invisible things are like two sides of the same coin; they become actualized through mutual interference. By *visualizing the invisible*, we want to provide a new awareness of scenery that we normally take for granted.

ARCHITECTURE AS FURNITURE, FURNITURE AS ARCHITECTURE

Is there a boundary line between furniture and architecture? Normally, the study of form and space is done with a model as the base. It is easy to experiment intuitively with a model by turning it upside down or partially breaking it. There are also many different scales you can use for the same space, such as 1:1000 to see the entire site or 1:1 to study the details. It makes you wonder about the distinction between furniture and architecture as you repeatedly move your point of view by alternately pulling back or approaching to look at the model.
By treating them as two separate areas of expertise, you might be reducing their potential. With this viewpoint in mind, we attempt to approach from both directions by designing furniture as though it were architecture and designing architecture as though it were furniture. In order to spatialize furniture and have architecture approach the human body, we would like to change the relationship between people, furniture and architecture with furniture that becomes for people, as it were, an extension of their own personal space, and architecture that fits closely together with people's behavior.

LEAVING SPACE

Regardless of whether we are dealing with architecture or products, we are conscious of *leaving space* to engage visitors and users. It is possible to encourage two-way communication between people as well as between people and a space or product by setting aside space which encourages people to actively participate, provides the freedom to customize everything, creates a narrative that everyone can easily relate to, and offers the flexibility to absorb information selectively. By not just accepting things passively, perhaps you can make discoveries or create a developmental method that surpasses the expectations and imagination of the creator. Our goal is to produce areas with spaces that only reach completion when people become involved.

SETTING THE SITE

Each site possesses its own strong characteristics that operate on the architecture standing there. Architectural design begins with analysis and study of the site. While on the one hand products enjoy the freedom of having no fixed user or location, on the other hand this lack of fixed conditions caused us to feel some uncertainty. By assigning our own conditions for mobile products through the selection of usage areas and circumstances within a site, we thought that we could incorporate these circumstances into the design. Building store fixtures and residential furniture in a manner similar to the relationship between a site and its architecture naturally imbues them with definite characteristics and personality. We treat architecture and its environment or products and the space they occupy more as one object by *setting the site*.

INSPIRED BY MATERIALS

We are attracted to building materials and furniture frames that we see at architecture sites and factories. We anticipate not just the raw materials before they give shape to an object or the strength of the grain before finishing a piece of furniture, but also the possibilities that change greatly according to the manufacturing process. Adding to the visual texture of raw materials, there are other physical properties such as the feel of materials when you touch them, the weight, and the firmness. You can find new ways to approach raw materials that surpasses their potential image by examining their texture, physical properties, and image rather than dealing with them only on a superficial level. Perhaps we can also treat formless things such as air and water as raw materials if we broaden our perspective. We explore the potential of being *inspired by materials* in the same way that we would decide what to cook depending on what ingredients we have on hand.

TORAFU'S SMALL CITY PLANNING

Wouldn't it be possible to change a city with one piece of furniture placed on the street? When we talk about urban planning, we tend to think of large-scale things like decisions about the boundaries and uses of land and infrastructure planning to connect these together. We believe that *small city planning* offers a new way to perceive a city by reducing the scale and thinking from the perspective of objects, furniture, and nearby communities. Through the gradual accumulation of such small experiments, we want to create the kind of mechanism that makes people feel greater affection for their city. If people are interested in architecture, then the whole town appears to be a museum of architecture; if people go for a stroll with an illustrated book on plants in one hand, then the entire town will seem like a botanical garden. For instance, if a community kitchen were to pop up in a public park, the park itself would feel like an open air dining hall, thereby feeding into the sense of shared ownership of the city. We want to turn cities into even more fulfilling places to live by reframing how people relate to the existing urban landscape. We believe that *small city planning* that changes awareness and viewpoints, creates a point of contact with the city, and takes into consideration the daily life environment would contribute greatly towards changing the city itself.

目次 Contents

はじめに Introduction p.1

モノから風景をつくる CREATING SCENERY FROM OBJECTS p.26

テンプレート イン クラスカ TEMPLATE IN CLASKA p.28

NIKE 1LOVE p.38

時間を取り込む CAPTURING TIME p.52

港北の住宅 HOUSE IN KOHOKU p.54

AKQA Tokyo Office p.68

gold wedding ring p.78

ドールハウスチェア dollhouse chair p.84

見えないものを可視化する VISUALIZING THE INVISIBLE p.90

空気の器 airvase p.92

光の織機 Light Loom（Canon Milano Salone） p.104

ガリバーテーブル Gulliver Table p.118

CMYK p.130

家具のような建築、建築のような家具
ARCHITECTURE AS FURNITURE, FURNITURE AS ARCHITECTURE p.132

コロロデスク／コロロスツール koloro-desk / koloro-stool p.134

目黒本町の住宅 HOUSE IN MEGUROHONCHO p.144

大岡山の住宅 HOUSE IN OOKAYAMA p.162

Big T p.174

余白をつくる LEAVING SPACE p.194

トラフのオバケ屋敷は"化かし屋敷"（東京都現代美術館）
TORAFU's Haunted house is a "Haunted play house"
（MUSEUM OF CONTEMPORARY ART TOKYO） p.196

ワンモック wanmock p.210

ゼロ・アワー 東京ローズ最後のテープ "ZERO HOUR" TOKYO ROSE'S LAST TAPE p.220

MOTOMI KAWAKAMI CHRONICLE 1966-2011 p.224

敷地を与える SETTING THE SITE p.230

キャッチボウル Catch-bowl p.232

クローブン clopen p.236

cobrina p.242

素材から発想する INSPIRED BY MATERIALS p.248

tapehook p.250

Y150 NISSAN パビリオン Y150 NISSAN PAVILION p.256

NIKE JMC p.258

LIGHT LIGHT DESK p.270

ミナ ペルホネン コティ minä perhonen koti p.272

water balloon p.278

イソップ Aesop p.282

トラフの小さな都市計画 TORAFU'S SMALL CITY PLANNING p.300

DŌZO BENCH p.304

NANYODO SHELF p.308

Run Pit by au Smart Sports p.312

WORLD CUP（みちのおくの芸術祭 山形ビエンナーレ）

WORLD CUP（YAMAGATA BIENNALE） p.322

食と緑の空中庭園 Garden in the Sky: Greenery and Delights p.326

渋谷のラジオ SHIBUYANORADIO p.330

FREITAG Store Tokyo p.338

FREITAG Store Tokyo Shibuya p.346

SLIDING NATURE（Panasonic Milano Salone） p.354

－石巻工房での実践－

FROM THEORY TO PRACTICE WITH ISHINOMAKI LABORATORY p.362

スカイデッキ SKYDECK p.366

AAスツール AA STOOL p.370

Rapha Mobile Cycle Club p.376

trees for everyone by Android p.380

3.11以後の建築／トラフ建築設計事務所＋石巻工房

Architecture since 3.11/

TORAFU ARCHITECTS + ISHINOMAKI LABORATORY p.382

こころの隙間に、知らぬまに建築を建ててしまうふたり 原 研哉

Two men building architecture that finds its way into your heart:

Kenya Hara p.388

作品データ Data on works p.398

略歴 Profile p.402

クレジット Credits p.412

CREATING SCENERY FROM OBJECTS

TEMPLATE IN CLASKA
NIKE 1LOVE

テンプレート イン クラスカ
TEMPLATE IN CLASKA
Tokyo／2004

東京・目黒の老朽化したホテルをリノベーションし、2003年にオープンしたホテルクラスカ。いくつかある客室の内、長期滞在者のための3室の改装を手掛けた。各部屋それぞれに、アーティストの絵画を掛けること、ロボットペットのアイボを設置することが条件であった。そこで、絵画やアイボ、ホテルの備品、宿泊者の持ち物など、さまざまな形や大きさの物を緩やかに規定するために、"テンプレート"をモチーフに穴を穿った1枚の薄い壁面を提案した。まったく性質の異なる要素を、テンプレート上に収納することで等価に扱い、モノから空間全体の風景をつくり出した。

An old hotel located in Meguro, Tokyo was renovated and reopened as CLASKA in 2003. We were approached to design three rooms for long-term guests out of the many rooms available at the hotel. The project brief called for an AIBO pet robot and artwork by Japanese artists in each room. Since the objects found in the room, such as artwork, AIBO, room furniture and guest's belongings, etc., are of all different sizes and shapes, holes cut in a thin wall create a template in which all items are displayed. This template creates an immersive scenery from these objects by equalizing the various elements stored within.

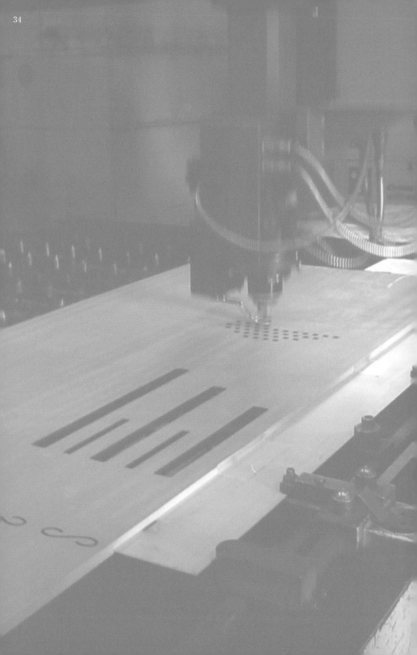

テンプレートの壁面は
レーザーカットにより精密に加工した。

The template wall was manufactured
with precision using a laser cutter.

壁面の内部は、テトリスのように
8つのブロックに分けて現場に搬入し、再度組み上げた。

The interior of the wall was divided in 8 blocks
which resemble the ones in a game of Tetris
to be transported and reassembled on site.

NIKE 1LOVE
Tokyo／2007

NIKEのAir Force1（AF1）というシューズを専門に扱った、1年間限定のストア。毎月増えていく新商品は最終的に300足近くになるため、その過程を視覚的に楽しめる空間が求められた。二重にしたガラスのシリンダー状のショーケースに並べられた真っ白いAF1は、ニューモデルがリリースされるたびに順次入れ替えられる。ショーケースに同じ向きで展示されるシューズは、水族館の水槽の中を回遊する魚の群れのようにも見える。商品であるシューズを空間の構成要素のひとつとして一体的に考えた。

NIKE 1LOVE was a temporary store open for one year specializing in NIKE's Air Force 1 (AF1) line of shoes. Since the number of shoes was to increase each month to about 300 pairs one year later, deliverables included a space where visitors could visually enjoy the process. We designed a double-glass cylindrical showcase in which white AF1 shoes would be replaced by new models as they are released. The shoes facing the same direction look like a migratory school of fish swimming in the tank of an aquarium. Thus, the AF1 shoe, which is the featured product, can be conceived of as an integral part of its surroundings.

オープニング時には、絵本のスイミーに見立てて、黒いAF1を1足だけディスプレイした。

We paid tribute to Swimmy, the children's book character, by inserting one black AF1 shoe in the display on opening day.

シューズを載せる高透過ガラスの棚板は
紫外線で硬化する接着剤で固定し、透明度を保った。

The shoes are mounted on high transmittance
glass shelves fixed with a bond
that hardens under ultraviolet light
to make the display transparent.

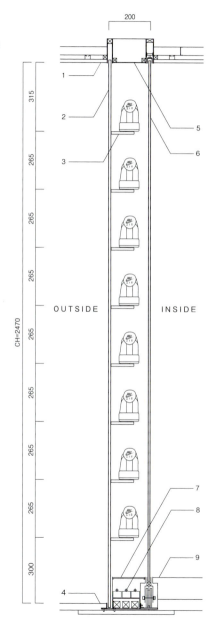

DETAILED SECTION

1 木毛セメント板：t=15mm
　AEP白塗装ツヤ無し
2 透明ガラス：t=12mm
3 高透過ガラスブラケット：t=12mm
4 床モルタル金ゴテ仕上げ：t=35mm
5 ステンレス鏡面仕上げ：t=1.5mm
6 引き戸透明ガラス：t=10mm
7 乳半アクリル：t=5mm
8 曲げFL蛍光管
9 スタイロフォーム下地 モルタル金ゴテ仕上げ：t=100mm

2階の予約制のラウンジでは
水面に見立てた床の開口から下階が見える。

The store can be seen through
an opening in the floor of the lounge
above (reservations only),
as if standing over water.

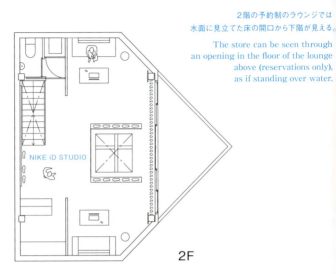

2F

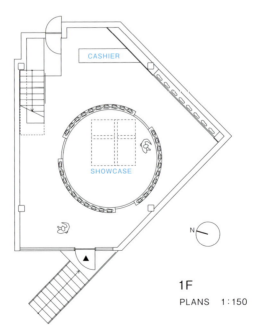

1F
PLANS 1:150

時間を取り込む

CAPTURING TIME

HOUSE IN KOHOKU

AKQA Tokyo Office

gold wedding ring

dollhouse chair

港北の住宅
HOUSE IN KOHOKU
Kanagawa／2008

横浜の高台にある閑静な住宅地。施主の夫婦は長年住み慣れたこの場所に、小さくも明るい平屋の住居を希望した。敷地は、住宅が密集した北向き勾配の斜面で、ひな壇状に高い南側隣地には2階建ての建物があり、南面からの採光は期待できない。そこで、個々にトップライトをもつ異形の筒型屋根が方々を向くことで、プライバシーを保ちながら光を採り入れる計画とした。屋根の稜線は、雨水を受け流すと同時に内部へも直接現れ、空間を柔らかく分節する。切り取られた空には流れる雲が垣間見え、自然環境の変化を絶えず映し込み、季節や時間によって変わる、射し込む光の表情が空間を変容させる。

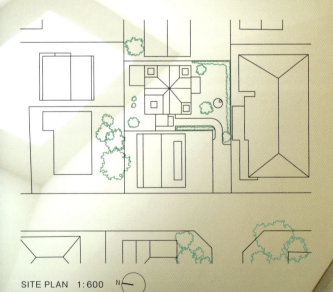

SITE PLAN 1:600

This house is located in Yokohama in a quiet residential area sitting on a hill. The clients, a married couple who has lived in this area for a long time, wanted a small but sun-bathed one-story house. Since the site is tilted to the north, and the neighboring house to the south is two-storied and built on a tiered, higher ground, it seemed almost impossible to let in light from the south. However, by reorienting the tube-shaped windows on the roof, we were able to let in light while protecting the clients' privacy. While the ridges in the roof help evacuate rainwater, the resulting arris in the ceiling is visible from the inside, where it creates a soft separation. The changes of nature are constantly projected in the top-lights through which fleeting clouds can be seen. Thus, the appearance of the interior changes as the brightness and softness of light does according to season and time of day.

BEDROOM

LIVING ROOM

KITCHEN

ENTRANCE

PLAN 1:100   N

SECTION

AKQA Tokyo Office
Tokyo / 2015

クリエイティブエージェンシー、AKQAの東京オフィスの内装計画。ビルの地下1階にあることを感じさせない明るさと、天井高6mの大空間を活かし、同社のクリエイティビティをアピールできるオフィスが求められた。既存躯体の高低差を利用してゾーニングし、大樹のある中庭を中心に諸機能を配置する回遊動線で、一体感をもたせる計画とした。中庭に敷き詰めた白い玉砂利を室内まで延長し、外光を反射させることで内部空間に取り込んだ。既存建物がもつ表情と形状的な特徴を計画の中に取り込み、新旧の要素を一体的に扱っている。

We performed the interior design for the Tokyo office of AKQA, a global ideas and innovation company. We strived to create an environment that puts forward the company's creativity while using the site's open spaces, six meter high ceilings and natural lighting to compensate for the office being located on the first basement floor. Centered around an inner court with big trees, we sought to capitalize on the site's existing leveled topography, to create distinct zones, and a circling line of flow, to bring a sense of unity to their various functionalities. Moreover, the white gravel extending indoors from the inner court diffuses natural light and brings it into the office. A balance between new and old was attained by integrating the expressivity and structural features of the existing building's frame into our design.

既存コンクリート床の表面を削り出すことで
骨材の断面が現れ、光沢のある素材感として生まれ変わった。

The surface of the existing concrete floors was polished
to expose the bare material and reveal its luster.

gold wedding ring
2012

身に着けているうちに表情が変わっていく結婚指輪のデザイン。ゴールドの上にシルバーで薄く
コーティングを施したシンプルな形のリングは、時間の経過と共にゴールドの地肌が見えてくる。
表情の変化で、ふたりが共有してきた時間を感じることができる。

This wedding ring gradually changes its appearance as it is worn. Coated on the
surface of a simple ring is a thin layer of silver that wears off to gradually reveal the
gold beneath as time goes by. The time shared between two people can thus be felt
by witnessing the changes in its appearance.

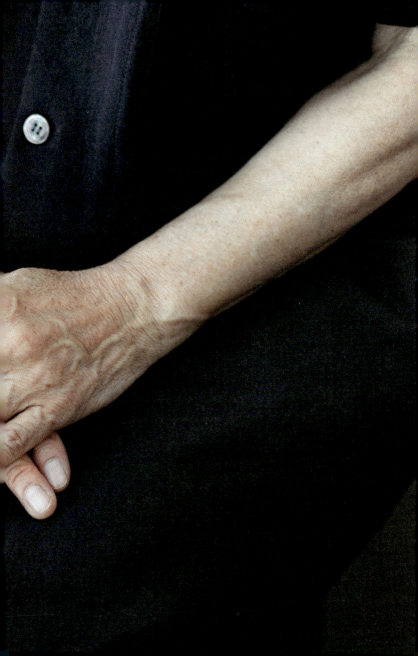

ドールハウスチェア
dollhouse chair
2014

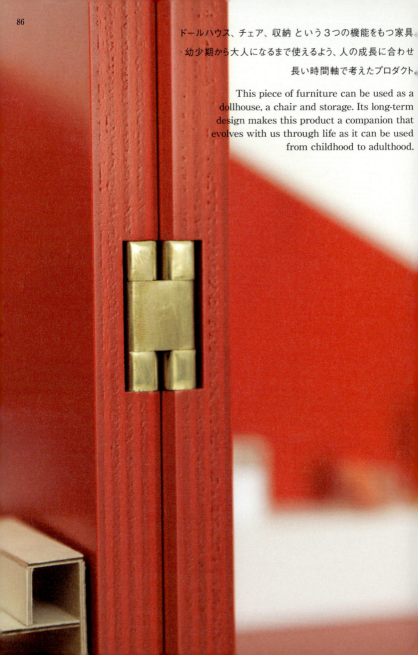

ドールハウス、チェア、収納 という３つの機能をもつ家具。
幼少期から大人になるまで使えるよう、人の成長に合わせ
長い時間軸で考えたプロダクト。

This piece of furniture can be used as a dollhouse, a chair and storage. Its long-term design makes this product a companion that evolves with us through life as it can be used from childhood to adulthood.

見えないものを可視化する

VISUALIZING THE INVISIBLE

- airvase
- Light Loom (Canon Milano Salone)
- Gulliver Table
- CMYK

空気を包み込むように、形を自由に変えられる紙の器。1枚のフラットな紙に無数の切り込みがあり、広げ方によって、小皿や小鉢、花瓶など、用途に合わせて自由な形を作ることができる。薄くて軽く、立ち上げると張りと強度が出て、使わない時は畳んでおける。広げた器を手に取ると、空気そのものを持っているかのような感覚になる。

空気の器
airvase
2010

This is a paper bowl that enfolds air by freely changing its shape. Presenting multiple slits, the airvase can be molded from a flat piece of paper into a dish, a small bowl or a vase according to the intended usage. The thin and lightweight paper gives strength and resistance as a container and allows it to be folded compactly when not in use. Taking the expanded vessel into one's hands creates the impression of holding air itself.

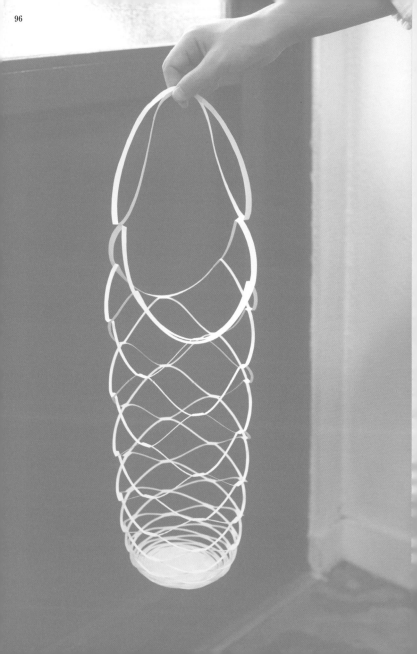

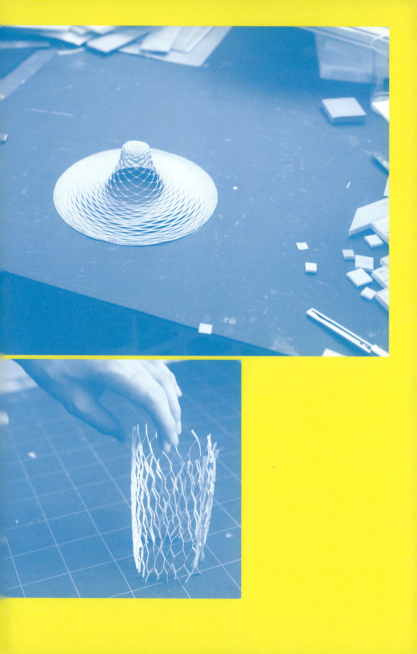

製作のきっかけとなった展覧会でトラフに与えられたテーマカラーの緑色を
片面を黄色、もう片面を青色とすることで、その混じり合いによって表現している。
最終的に金型で量産するまでは、手切りによる実験と検討を重ねた。
同心円状に 10mm 間隔で切り込みを入れるところから始め
限界値の 0.9mm 間隔の切り込みで自立する形ができ上がった。

During an exhibition, we were given green as a theme color,
which prompted us to express it as the combination of yellow and blue on each side
of a single sheet of paper. Each prototype was hand-cut until we were finally able to
mass-produce the airvase using a metal die, and what began as a series of concentric slits
at intervals of 10mm, became a free-standing structure with slits at intervals of 0.9mm.

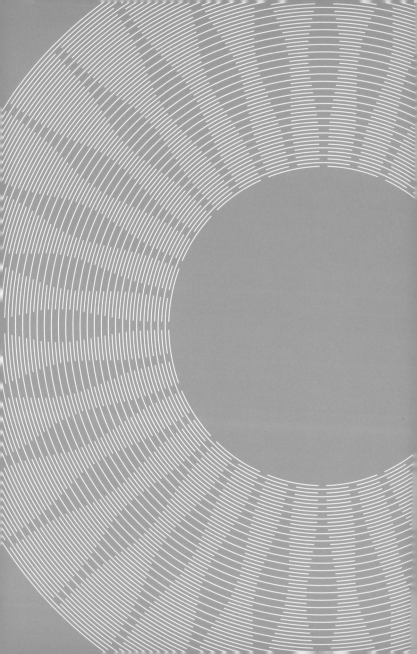

光の織機

Light Loom (Canon Milano Salone)
Milano, Italy / 2011

「ミラノサローネ」での、キヤノンの展示会場構成。デジタルイメージング技術を駆使した、新しい映像空間が求められた。暗闇のちりが照らされると"光の形"が見えるように、もともと実体のない光が目の前に現れる時、光との新しい関係が築けると考えた。プロジェクターから放射状に放たれる光の形を無数の水糸でトレースすることで、光を擬似的に実体化した。糸がつくる錐体は、映像スクリーンとなって空間を横断する。糸が絶え間なく動く光を捉え、光や映像が空間に織り込まれたかのような一体感によって、虚構とも現実ともつかない、新たなリアリティーを体感できる。

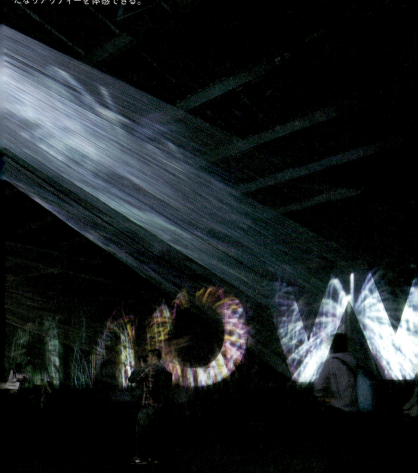

We were invited to design the Canon exhibition site at the "Milano Salone."
The installation was to include the application of the company's digital imaging technology. We were influenced by how light, normally intangible, can appear as *light forms* before the spectators' very eyes when dust is illuminated in the dark. We wanted to build a new relationship with light, so by tracing the light beams radiating from the projectors with countless strings, the light is artificially given substance. The resulting cone of strings creates an image screen that stretches across the space. These strings appear to capture the constantly moving light, weaving it inside the space. A new reality can be experienced through the unity of light and images, blending together a space that is neither virtual nor real.

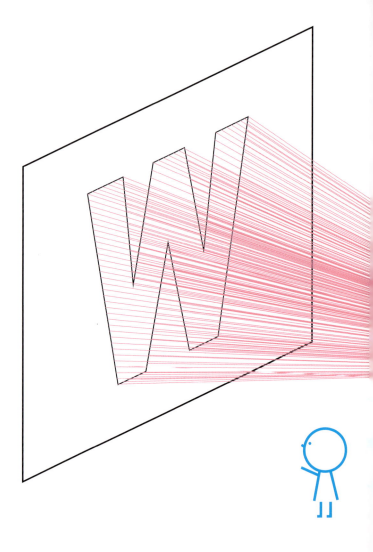

Light is projected from a projector onto a beam of suspended strings.

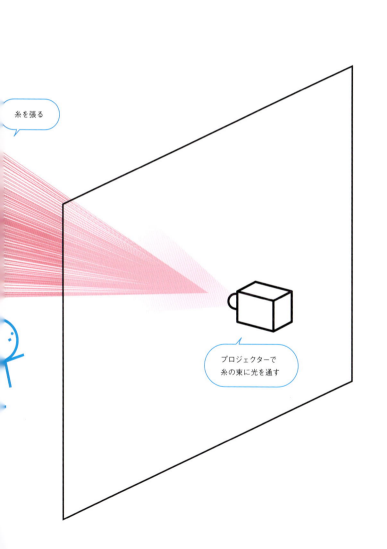

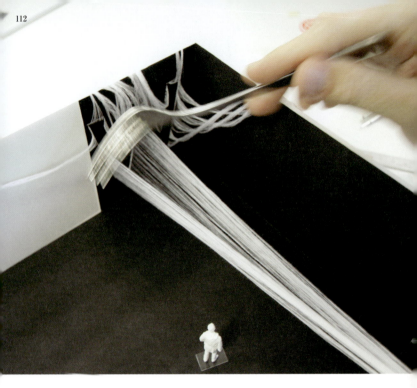

放射状の糸の束に映像がどのように映し出されるかを検証するため
模型や原寸大での実験を繰り返した。

Various scale and actual-size simulations were conducted
to test how images could be projected
onto a beam of radiating strings.

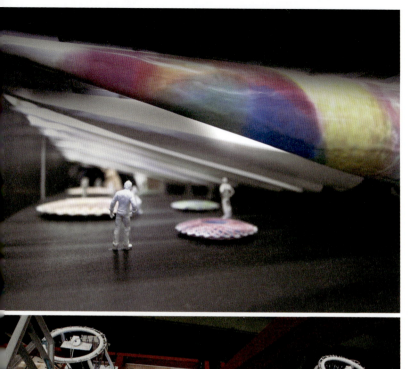

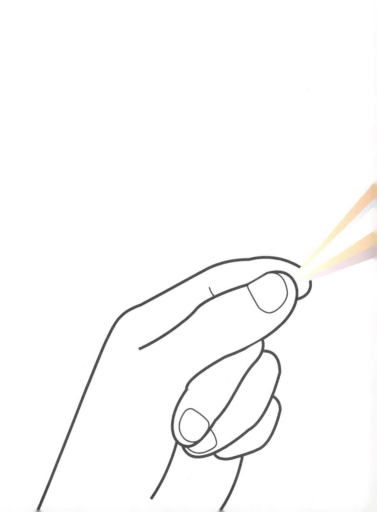

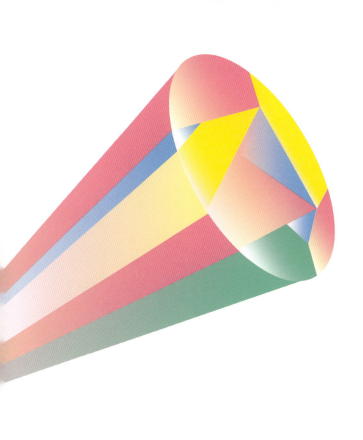

ガリバーテーブル
Gulliver Table
Tokyo／2011

東京ミッドタウンの芝生広場で開催された、「Midtown DESIGN TOUCH Park」におけるインスタレーションの計画。緩やかな斜面の芝生広場に水平線を引くように、一直線に幅5m、長さ50mの長いテーブルを設置した。斜面との関係で自然と高さが変わるこのテーブルは、床であり、ベンチであり、遊具であり、屋根でもある。さまざまな人が、おのおのに場所を発見しながら、まるで大家族の食卓のように、ひとつのテーブルを囲む。このテーブルが基準線となり、広場に緩やかな勾配があることに気付く。

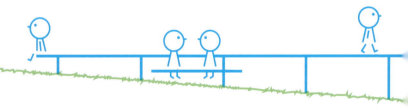

This installation was designed for the "Midtown DESIGN TOUCH Park" held in a wide open grass field in Tokyo Midtown. We installed a tabletop 50 meters long by 5 meters wide running in a straight line, as if drawing a horizontal line on the gently sloping grassy field. The table naturally grows taller as we move along the inclined plane and serves as a floor, a table, a bench, a playground or even a shelter. Various persons come together like a big family gathered around a single picnic table, discovering various places along the way. Furthermore, the table acts as a reference line that reveals the gentle slope in the topography.

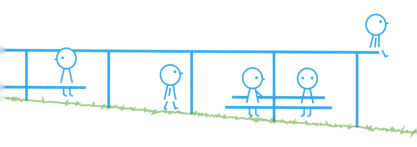

CMYK
2008

We were approached to design a futsal ball as part of MAGIS Japan's PR campaign. A typical soccer ball consists of an assembly of black pentagonal faces and white hexagonal faces. By combining Cyan (C), Magenta (M) and Yellow (Y) in equal parts we obtain Black (K), or Key. To illustrate this principle, we designed a ball that looks as if the colored pentagons have shifted from the impact of a kick. We decided to bring our own touch to the traditional black and white ball and revamp its design for the occasion.

家具ブランドMAGIS JapanのPR用に、フットサルボールのデザインを手掛けた。一般的なサッカーボールは、黒い五角形と白い六角形で構成される。シアン（C）、マゼンタ（M）、イエロー（Y）を同比で混ぜると黒（K）ができる混色の原理を使い、まるでボールを蹴った勢いで五角形のパターンがずれてしまったかのようにデザインした。見慣れた白黒のボールに少し手を加えて、いつもとは違う視点を与えたいと考えた。

家具のような
建築、
建築のような
家具

ARCHITECTURE
AS FURNITURE,
FURNITURE
AS ARCHITECTUR

koloro-desk / koloro-stool

HOUSE IN MEGUROHONCHO

HOUSE IN OOKAYAMA

Big T

コロロデスク／コロロスツール
koloro-desk / koloro-stool
2012

化粧板メーカー伊千呂の、カラフルなポリエステル化粧板を使った家具。顔を突っ込むと部屋のような感覚がもてるデスクを提案した。誰にも邪魔されない個室のように使うことができ、小窓を開けて光や風景を採り込んだり、照明を付けたり、鉢植えを置くなど、自室を模様替えする感覚でアレンジできる。人の居場所をつくるこのデスクは、空間化した家具とも言える。

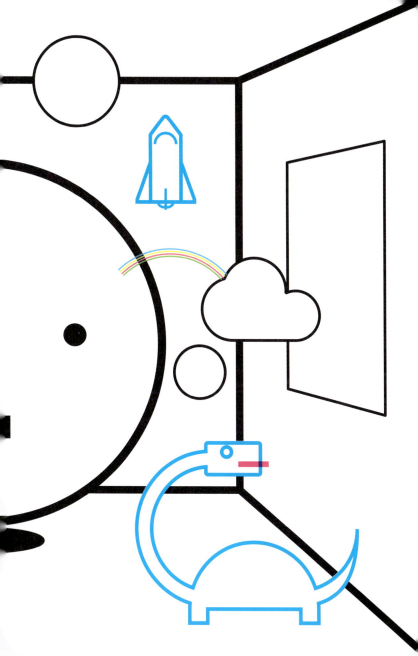

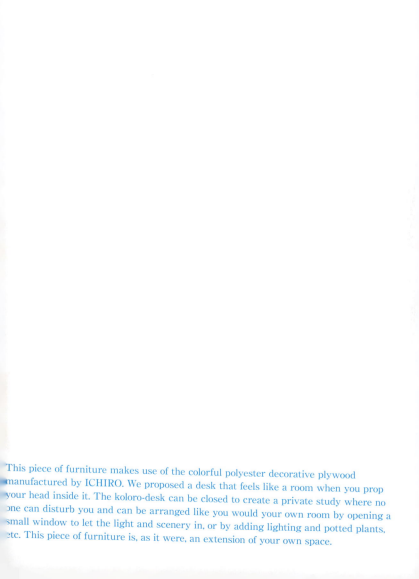

This piece of furniture makes use of the colorful polyester decorative plywood manufactured by ICHIRO. We proposed a desk that feels like a room when you prop your head inside it. The koloro-desk can be closed to create a private study where no one can disturb you and can be arranged like you would your own room by opening a small window to let the light and scenery in, or by adding lighting and potted plants, etc. This piece of furniture is, as it were, an extension of your own space.

築40年経つRC造のビルのリノベーション。3階を住居、それ以外が事務所と倉庫として使われていたビルの、2階と3階の住居及び外装を改修した。外部階段でしか上下階の行き来ができない既存建物に、内部動線として3階中央の床に穴を開け、その真下に階段を組み込んだ大きな家具を置いた。家具のスケールをひとまわり大きくしたこのボックス状の家具が、書斎や寝室、個室など、周囲に性格の違う場所を生み出しながら、大きな気積を緩やかに仕切っている。

目黒本町の住宅
HOUSE IN MEGUROHONCHO
Tokyo／2012

This is a renovation project of a 40-year-old reinforced concrete building with residential spaces on the 3rd floor and storage and office spaces below.
We renovated the building's exterior and living quarters on the 2nd and 3rd floors. An aperture was made at the center of the 3rd floor and a large piece of furniture with built-in stairs was placed directly underneath it to create a line of flow inside the building and connect the upper and lower floors which were previously accessible by stairs on the exterior of the existing building. By being one order bigger than the furniture around it, the box-shaped stairwell loosely partitions the large volume of the building, thus creating spaces with different personalities around it, such as a study, a bedroom or a private room, etc.

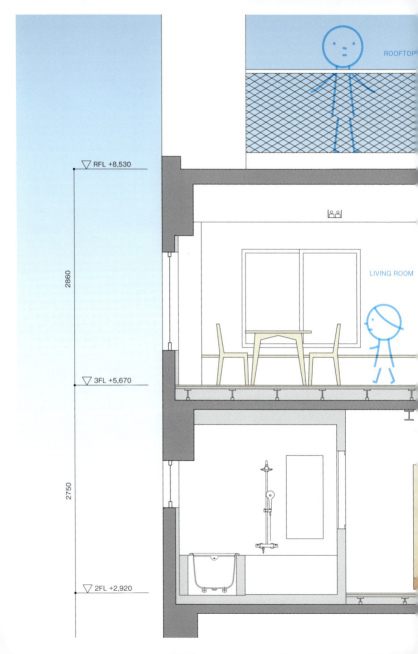

ボックス状の家具の上の大きな踊り場が
もうひとつの小さな階となるなど、空間構成を担う存在となっている。

Atop of this box-shaped piece of furniture is a wide landing
that makes another small floor,
thus acting as a structural element.

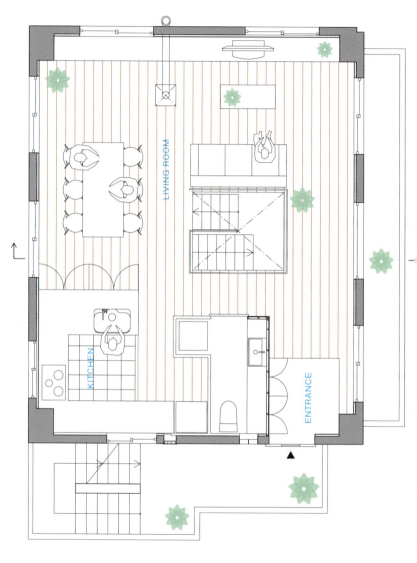

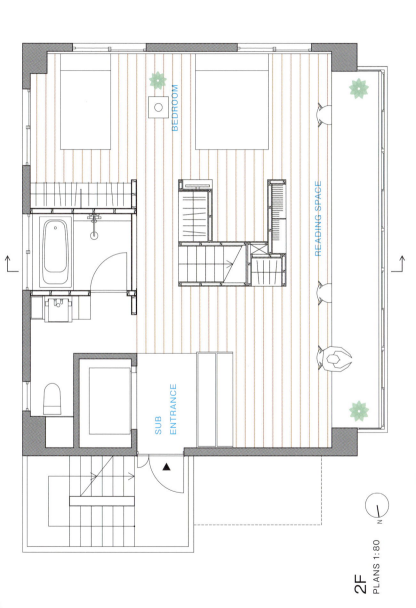

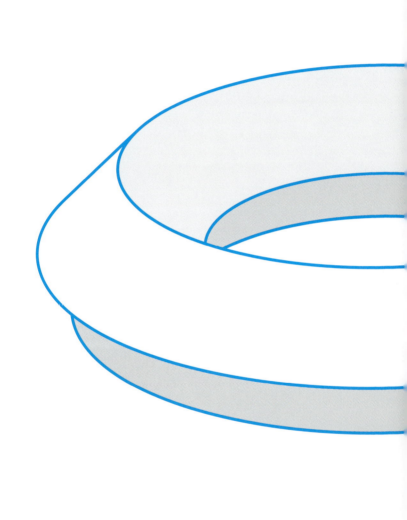

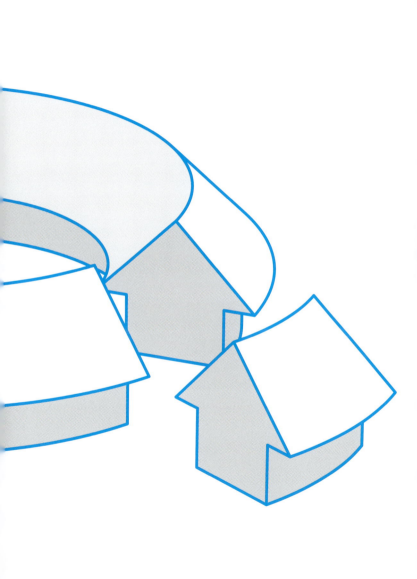

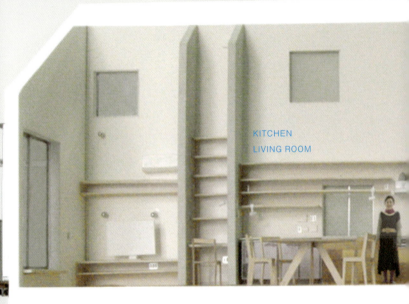

大岡山の住宅
HOUSE IN OOKAYAMA
Tokyo／2010

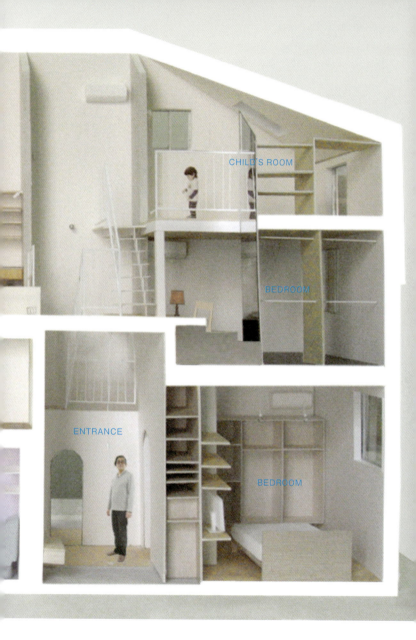

SITE PLAN 1 : 1000

東京の住宅地に建つ、木造3階建ての二世帯住宅の計画。間口4.7m、奥行き16.5mの細長い敷地で、周囲3方に隣地建物が近接するため、斜線規制による最大容積を確保しながら間口の狭さを感じさせないことが課題となった。間口を狭めてしまう廊下をなくすため、中央に玄関と階段を配置し、寝室とパブリック空間を南北に分割する平面計画とした。リビングの床の段差を利用したテーブル、ベンチにもなる出窓、4枚の耐力壁を利用したデスクや棚など建築の部位を家具化する。建築があって家具を置く、という順序ではなく、同時に考えることで間口の狭い空間を有効に使った。

Two generations live in this three-storied wooden house located in a Tokyo residential area. The site corresponds to a 4.7m wide by 16.5 m long fringe of land that is enclosed by buildings on three sides. Our goal was to alleviate the impression of narrowness of the frontage within the maximum volume allowed by setback restrictions. To eliminate the cramping effect of a corridor on the frontage, we devised a level plan placing the entrance and stairs at the center while dividing the bedroom and public areas on a north-south axis. Architectural features become furniture by using the difference in level in the living room floor to make a table, the bay window to make a bench or the four sturdy walls as a desk and shelves. We were able to make the best use of the site's narrow frontage by thinking of the building and furniture in a simultaneous, rather than sequential, order.

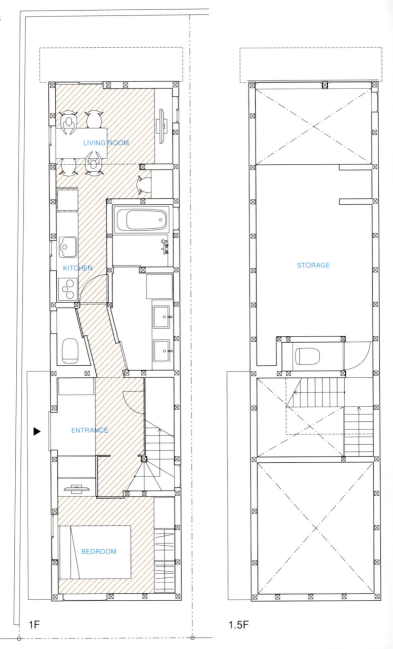

PLANS 1:100

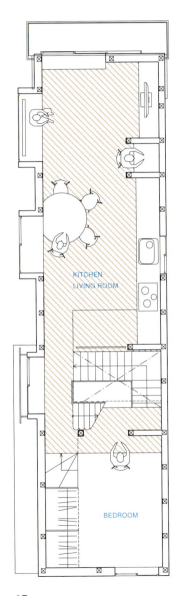

2F

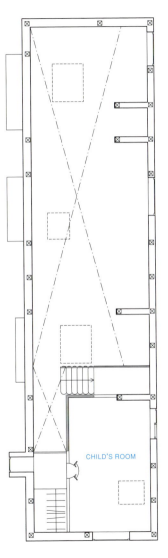

3F

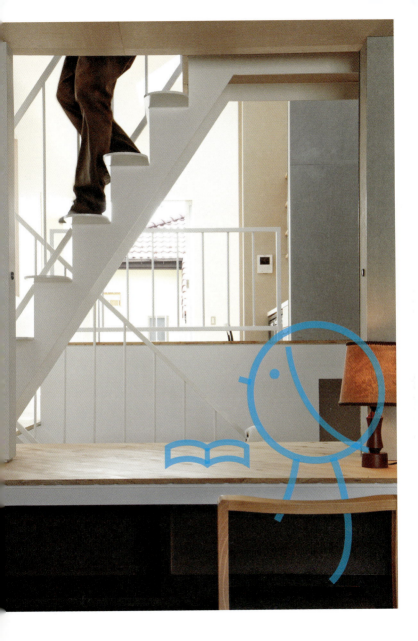

広大な原野に建つ、夫婦とゲストのための週末住宅。住居棟と、テニスコートや大浴場のあるレクリエーション棟とをT字型に連結し、群生する白樺の風景を取り込むように敷地の東側に配置した。農業用倉庫の外郭で大きな空間を確保し、住まうために必要な諸室を分棟として入れ子状に配置した。建物外郭とは切り離して独立した構造体とすることで、冬場の厳しい環境の中で断熱性能を高めている。大きな気積の中に、建築とまではいかない中間的なスケールの大きな家具を配置するような感覚で、必要諸室を配置した。室の内外に場をつくる、おおらかな空間を目指した。

Big T

A weekend house built on a wide field for married couples and guests. Connected in a T-shaped layout, the residential and recreation buildings, which feature tennis courts and a large public bath, are situated on the east side of the grounds in order to afford a view of the many Japanese white birch trees that grow there. The farm storehouse enclosure ensures a large space, and all the rooms that are essential for living are installed as separate blocks. Insulation efficiency is improved during harsh winter weather by keeping the independent structure away from the building enclosure. The essential rooms were placed as though they were moderately large pieces of furniture to be installed in this wide open space. Our goal was to create a broad space both inside and outside of these rooms.

2階のテラスからゴルフの打ち放しができるように
建物を東側に寄せ、敷地にも余白をもたせた。

There is a line of flow outside each room
where families and guests can gather.

農業用倉庫の骨組みを使って
大きな内部空間を確保した中に
木造の諸室を点在させる。

The wood construction rooms dot
the large interior space offered
by the farm storehouse building frame.

There is a line of flow outside each room where families and guests can gather.

余白をつくる

LEAVING SPACE

TORAFU's Haunted house is a "Haunted play house"
(MUSEUM OF CONTEMPORARY ART TOKYO)
wanmock
"ZERO HOUR" TOKYO ROSE'S LAST TAPE
MOTOMI KAWAKAMI CHRONICLE 1966-2011

トラフのオバケ屋敷は"化かし屋敷"(東京都現代美術館)
TORAFU's Haunted house is a "Haunted play house"
(MUSEUM OF CONTEMPORARY ART TOKYO)
Tokyo／2013

東京都現代美術館の子供向け展覧会「オバケと
パンツとお星さま」において、トラフは「オバケ屋敷」
を担当した。一見何の変哲もない壁の絵画には
裏側があり、鑑賞者を驚かす仕掛け部屋になって
いる。ここでは、鑑賞者は"化かされる"だけでなく、
仕掛け部屋に入った途端に"化かす"側となり、
額縁のこちら側と向こう側とで役割が入れ替わる。
双方向的なコミュニケーションの仕掛けを施し、
来場者が能動的に関わることのできる空間とした。

The Museum of Contemporary Art Tokyo presented an exhibition for children entitled "GHOSTS, UNDERPANTS and STARS" for which we designed a "Haunted house".
Hidden behind the paintings hanging on seemingly inconspicuous walls is in fact a backstage room from where all sorts of antics are unleashed on unsuspecting visitors. Museum-goers previously on the receiving end of such antics can also enter the secret room and reverse the roles by becoming in turn tricksters on the other side of the paintings. We aimed to create a space that engages visitors more actively by enabling two-way communication between them.

Inside Out

Inside
Out

絵画の裏側の仕掛け部屋。絵の中から手を出したり、顔を覗かせたり、鑑賞者を"化かす"ことができる。

Visitors can *spook* other visitors by popping out their hands and faces from behind the paintings.

ワンモック
wanmock
2012

デザイナー・原研哉氏ディレクションの「犬のための建築」展でデザインしたDIY家具。飼い主の服の匂いと布の触り心地が犬を安心させることから、木のフレームにかぶせた飼い主の古着がハンモックのように犬の体を包み込む。ソファに座る飼い主が手を伸ばせば犬と触れ合うことができ、犬との距離を縮める。使う人それぞれに個性を与えることができる「犬のための建築」は、人間と犬の心地よい関係を生み出す。

コピーライター・糸井重里氏の愛犬ブイヨンが
洋服の上に座る写真に着想を得て
飼い主の服を使うアイデアが生まれた。

The idea of using the owner's garments
came from a picture of copywriter Shigesato Itoi's
beloved dog "Bouillon" sitting on his clothes.

We designed this DIY piece of furniture as part of the "Architecture for Dogs" project directed by designer Kenya Hara. Since the smell of its owner and the touch of fabric make the dog feel at ease, we covered a wooden frame with the clothes of its owner so the garment wraps around the dog's body in the same way as a hammock. Owners can reach out and touch their dogs easily from their sofa, bringing them closer to each other. "wanmock", a piece of architecture for dogs which can be personalized, makes the relationship between humans and dogs even more enjoyable.

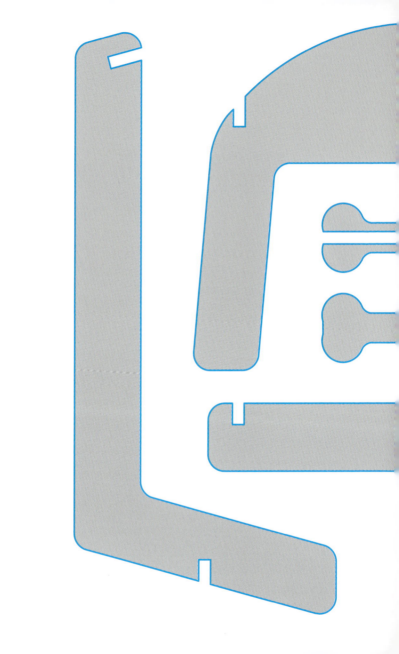

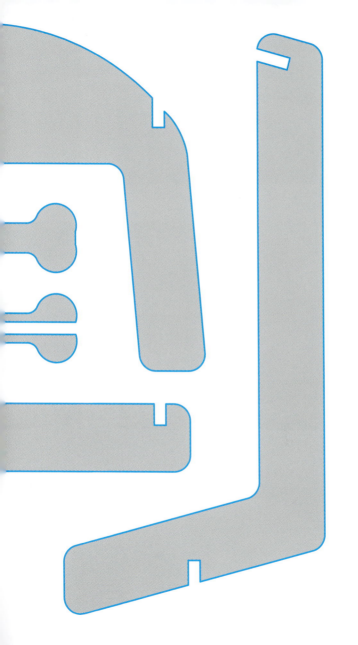

この図面を5倍に拡大印刷して15mmの板にあて、切り出して組み立てるとフレームが出来るワン！
By enlarging the blueprint 5 times, printing it onto a 15mm board, cutting it out and assembling it, my master can obtain a frame. Bowwow!

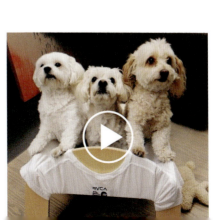

現代美術作家のやなぎみわ氏が脚本、演出、美術を手掛けた公演の舞台装置。太平洋戦争中のラジオ番組のスタジオが舞台で、劇中に登場する女性アナウンサーのカウンターが求められた。このカウンターは5等分されていて、開演時はひとつのリングの形をしている。ストーリーの展開と共に演者自身が配置換えをすることで、さまざまな情景を観客に連想させるツールとなる。

ゼロ・アワー 東京ローズ最後のテープ
"ZERO HOUR"
TOKYO ROSE'S LAST TAPE
Kanagawa, Aichi / 2013

We designed the set for "ZERO HOUR" TOKYO ROSE'S LAST TAPE, a production to which contemporary art artist Miwa Yanagi contributed script, direction and artwork. Deliverables included desks for female announcers appearing on the set of a radio program broadcast during World War II. The opening scene shows a ring-shaped counter that is then split into five parts which serve as tools suggesting various settings to the spectator as they are rearranged by the actresses according to the developments in the narrative.

望郷の念におとしいれ、
アメリカ軍の士気を低下させましたか？

MOTOMI KAWAKAMI
CHRONICLE 1966-2011
Tokyo／2011

デザイナー・川上元美氏の個展の会場構成。広範な作品群を振り返る展示で、1点1点の作品を丁寧に、また魅力的に来場者へ伝えることが課題となった。そこで、作品ごとに大小さまざまな四角いボックスで展示する構成とした。ボックス間の路地を、来場者が探索しながら作品とめぐり合い、これまでの活動を一緒に辿るような感覚を与える。来場者が選択的に情報を紡いでいける、柔軟な空間を目指した。

The venue layout for the exhibition dedicated to designer Motomi Kawakami which offers a retrospective glance at his extensive collection of works, was given careful consideration in order to determine how best to emphasize the beauty of each individual work for visitors. To do this, each work is displayed inside square-shaped boxes of varying sizes. As they walk down the lanes between these boxes, visitors were given the impression that they were tracing the evolution of Kawakami's career as they explored and encountered each work. We sought to create a flexible space where visitors could absorb information selectively.

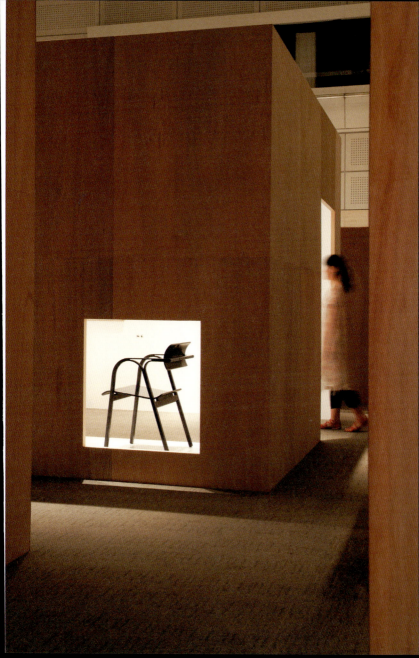

SETTING THE SITE

Catch-bowl

clopen

cobrina

キャッチボウル
Catch-bowl
2011

どんな部屋にも必ずある、コーナーに着目したシェルフの提案。ひとつの半球をケーキのように4分の1と4分の3に切り分けると、一方はちょうど入隅に、もう一方は出隅にフィットする。高さを調節し、まるで運動会の玉入れのように物を入れることができる、楽しくて軽快なシェルフを考えた。コーナーを"敷地"に見立てることで、空間と家具をより一体的なものとして捉えられる。

We proposed a shelf, focusing on corners, which inevitably exist in every room. When a hemisphere is divided into a quarter and three quarters, the quarter snugly fits into a concave corner and the three quarters onto a convex corner. Based on this idea, we created a joyful and lightsome shelf that allows the user to adjust its height and also use it as a bowl to enjoy putting things in it just like playing a ball toss game in an athletics festival. Therefore, using corners as an ad-hoc *site* enabled us to see space and furniture as one and the same.

クロープン
clopen
2012

壁から突き出た無垢材のオープン棚のように見える厚さ34mmの棚板は、アルミの精巧な内部構造をもつ引き出しになっている。突き板を練り付けた薄い構造体が、棚板の厚みの中に空間を生み出す。マグネットの鍵で木口を引くと、印鑑や通帳など、玄関先で貴重品を収納する秘密の引き出しが現れる。玄関という場所を"敷地"と捉え、使われるシーンも含めて考えた。

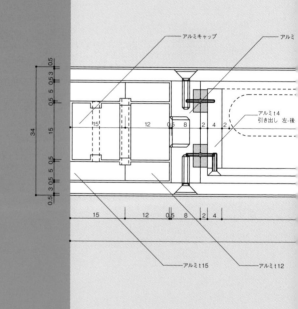

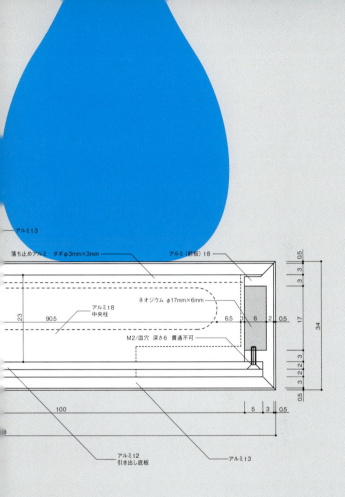

DETAILED SECTION 1:1

What appears to be a 34mm thick natural wood shelf sticking out of the wall is in fact a concealed drawer constructed from elaborate aluminum parts. Attaching sliced veneer to a thin structure, we made space between two boards which can be opened using magnetic keys. When pulled open, a secret drawer appears to store your valuables, such as seal and bankbooks, etc., without leaving the entrance. Therefore, thinking how to use the entrance way as a *site*, we imagined many usage scenarios.

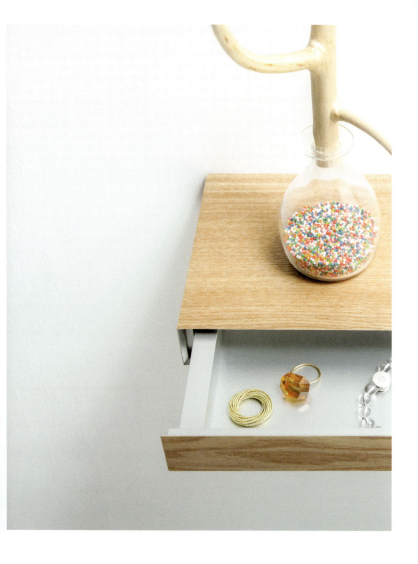

老舗家具メーカー飛騨産業との協働によって生まれた家具シリーズ。空間を広く使うことができる"こぶりな"家具をデザインした。天板の下に納まる背板の低い椅子や、壁に寄せることもできる円卓など、大きさだけではない、使い勝手におけるコンパクトさを追求している。日本における小さな部屋を"敷地"として捉え、間取りや使い方の変化に対応しやすい、軽やかな家具を目指した。

cobrina
2013

We designed a series of small-sized pieces of furniture that allow space to be used more effectively. The "cobrina" collection is the result of a collaboration with Hida Sangyo, a well-established furniture manufacturer in Japan. ("cobrina" derives from the Japanese expression *koburi-na* used to describe things that are smallish or undersized.) Whether it is the shorter chairs that can be stowed under the tabletop or its semicircular shape that sets close against the wall, compact furniture not only has an effect on size, but usability as well. By taking a small Japanese room as our *site*, we sought to create light furniture that can be easily rearranged or repurposed.

素材から発想する

INSPIRED BY MATERIALS

- tapehook
- Y150 NISSAN PAVILION
- NIKE JMC
- LIGHT LIGHT DESK
- minä perhonen koti
- water balloon
- Aesop

tapehook
2011

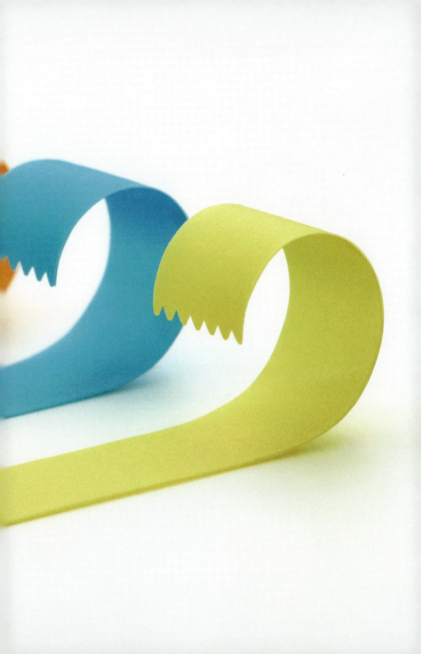

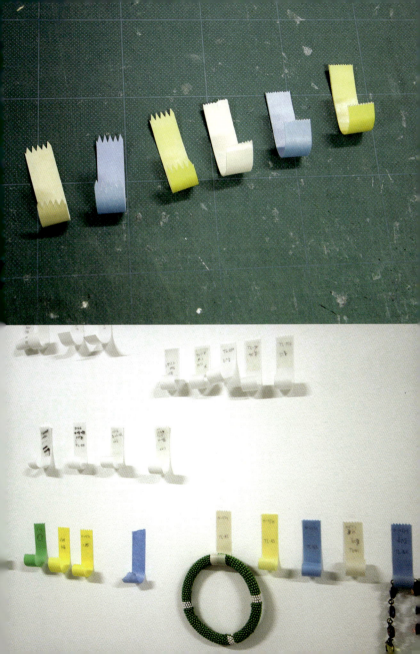

テープの巻き癖のような形状の紙製のフック。壁に貼ったマスキングテープをそのまま壁掛けのフックにできないかと考え、濡れた紙が乾くと強度をもつという紙の性質を利用した。紙を丸めて形を固定し、水に浸して乾燥させ、アクセサリーや鍵などが掛けられる強度をもたせた。紙の柔らかい印象とは相反する機能の意外性が、不思議な存在感を生んでいる。

This is a paper hook that looks like a curled tape. Since wet paper becomes stronger when dried, we wondered if we could use this property of paper to turn a piece of masking tape into a wall-mounted hook. Curling the tip of the paper, the hook is soaked then dried. This process gives it enough strength to hang small accessories or keys. The unpredictable resilience its appearance defies gives it an extraordinary presence.

Y150 NISSAN パビリオン
Y150 NISSAN PAVILION
Kanagawa／2009

横浜で開催された「開国博 Y150」における、NISSAN Y150 ドリームフロントの会場構成。日産自動車の環境活動を体現する空間が求められ、直径4.5〜10mの大小16個の気泡(バルーン)で大きな展示室を満たす計画とした。訪れた人は気泡の余白を縫うように回遊する。その表面には湾曲した像が映り込み、虚像が実体化したような印象を与える。気泡(図)が生み出す余白(地)を実空間として計画した。空気そのものを素材のひとつとして捉え、光や気配の浸透する空間を目指した。

We designed the NISSAN Y150 Dream Front pavilion as part of the EXPO Y150 initiative commemorating the 150th Anniversary of the Opening of the Port of Yokohama. Deliverables included a showcase of the company's environmental practices and a large exhibition space that houses 16 giant bubbles (balloons) ranging from 4.5m to 10m in diameter. These bubbles give the surrounding space its physicality, inviting visitors to playfully navigate through it. Curved images are projected onto the membranes giving virtual images the aspect of solidity. The room (ground) found between the bubbles (figure) is where real space is produced. Using air as a material, our concept aimed to create a space permeated by light and signs of presence.

東京湾岸エリアの倉庫街に位置する、NIKEの展示スペースとオフィス機能を併設する施設。季節ごとに開催される展示会のための大きなスペースを自社用に確保することと、もともと物流倉庫であった既存建物の特徴を活かした、スポーツブランドとしてアピールできる空間が求められた。体育館の吸音材や廃材フローリングの家具、床面のコートライン、大きな空間でも目立つスタジアムのようなサインなど、随所にスポーツにおける大空間のディテールを取り入れ、これらの素材がもつイメージにより、大きな空間全体にブランドの個性を浸透させた。

NIKE JMC
Tokyo／2009

向き合うように正対する、男女のトイレ扉のピクトサイン。
The pictograms on the men's and women's bathroom door are ready to face off.

We designed a facility located in the warehouse district of the Tokyo Bay area that accommodates the offices and exhibition space of NIKE. The project aimed to provide the resident sports apparel company with a large yet appealing space to be used year-round for in-house exhibitions while making the best use of the existing building's characteristics. Everywhere, we incorporated lofty details associated with sports with such elements as furniture made from acoustic material and scrap wood flooring sourced from sports arenas, court lines drawn on the floor, and big flashy signs, such as those found in stadiums. By making use of the image associated with these materials, we sought to give meaning to this expansive facility as a whole.

実際に体育館で使われていた
コートラインの描かれた
フローリング材をばらして
エントランス扉や家具の
天板に使用した。

The entrance door and
the tabletops of furniture
feature the court lines
from recycled flooring that
was actually used
in a sport arena.

スイスと日本のデザイナーが、両国の企業と共に取り組むデザインワークショップ「DESIGN WORKSHOP JAPAN-SWITZERLAND」で生まれたデスク。スイスの大手システム家具メーカー WOGG の通電可能なアルミサンドイッチパネルを用い、素材を活かした軽い構造に照明を内蔵したデスクを提案した。折り畳み可能で、チェアのように持ち運べる軽快さをもつ。

LIGHT LIGHT DESK
2015

This desk was conceived by Japanese and Swiss designers who engaged with local companies over the course of two Japan-Switzerland Design Workshops. We proposed a desk consisting of a light aluminum frame with a built-in LED light that makes use of energizable sandwich panels made by WOGG, a major systematized furniture manufacturer from Switzerland. The result is both lightweight and collapsible, and can easily be transported like a folding chair.

ミナ ペルホネン コティ
minä perhonen koti
Kanagawa ／2015

ファッションブランド・ミナ ペルホネンの、湘南 T-SITE 内にオープンした「ミナ ペルホネン コティ」の内装計画。店名のコティは家という意味をもち、ホームプロダクトを中心に取り扱う。床面はテキスタイルとボタンを敷き詰めてエポキシ樹脂で固め、一つひとつ覗き込みたくなるようなデザインとした。中央に置かれた島什器は、色鮮やかな床面が見えるよう、箱の高さを変えながら真鍮製のパイプ脚で軽やかに床から浮かせた。同ブランドを象徴するテキスタイルを、仕上げ材としてインテリアに取り込んだ。

エポキシ樹脂を3回に分けて流し込み
最終的には10mmの厚さとした。

Epoxy resin was applied three times
to obtain a 10mm thick veneer.

minä perhonen is a fashion brand and we performed the interior design for their shop "minä perhonen koti", which opened in the Shonan T-SITE mall. The name of the store *koti*, meaning house, derives from the fact that it handles everyday life items. The store floor is covered in textiles and buttons fixed with epoxy resin, which invites visitors to look at each one of them. We designed the island of fixtures found at the center of the store as to look light and appear to hover above the ground by using brass piping legs and varying the height of the compartments, to allow customers to look at the colorful textiles below. By doing so, we integrated the textiles symbolizing the minä perhonen brand into the store interior as a finishing material.

water balloon
2013

This lamp was designed in collaboration with a glass artist under the theme of *light*, and uses glass recycled from fluorescent lamps, which fell in disuse after the popularization of LED lights. This lighting equipment uses the optical properties of bubbles trapped in the recycled glass to reflect light diffusely. Each light bulb is handcrafted, giving it a charming shape; like a water balloon expanding out from the insulator socket,"water balloon"resulted from our desire to give salvaged materials new value.

"ヒカリ"をテーマに、ガラス作家とのコラボレーションによりデザインした照明。LED照明が普及することで不要となった、蛍光灯のリサイクルガラスを使用した。気泡混じりのリサイクルガラスの特性から、気泡に光を乱反射させる照明器具を考えた。手作業により一つひとつチャーミングな形をもつこの照明は、碍子ソケットから水風船がふくらんだようにも見える。再生材に新たな価値を与えたいと考えた。

OSB

OSB

Japanese cedar

Stainless steel

イソップ
Aesop
2012 -

オーストラリアのスキンケアブランド、イソップの店舗デザイン。店舗ごとに主な素材をひとつ決めてデザインしている。店内の什器に求められる機能は同じでも、素材の違いでつくりも変わり、多様なバリエーションを生み出してきた。周辺環境に対して店舗が引き立つような素材を選んだり、既存躯体の表情を素材と捉えるなど、素材やその扱い方は毎回異なる。

We performed the interior design for various stores by Aesop, an Australian skin care brand. Each design centered around one key material. Although the furniture was required to function the same way in each store, many variations arose and construction methods changed due to differences in materials. Considering a material for its capacity to make the store stand out from its surrounding environment or to accentuate an element of the existing structure meant different uses for different materials every time.

OSB

イソップ 新丸ビル店
Aesop Shin-Marunouchi
Tokyo ／ 2012

OSB

イソップ 横浜ベイクォーター店
Aesop Yokohama Bay Quarter
Kanagawa ／ 2012

Blackened steel

イソップ 渋谷店
Aesop Shibuya
Tokyo ／ 2013

Concrete

イソップ 河原町店
Aesop Kawaramachi
Kyoto ／ 2013

Japanese cedar

イソップ グランフロント大阪店
Aesop Grand Front Osaka
Osaka ／ 2014

Stainless steel

イソップ 東京ミッドタウン店
Aesop Midtown
Tokyo ／ 2015

Limestone

イソップ ニュウマン新宿店
Aesop NEWoMan Shinjuku
Tokyo ／ 2016

Japanese cedar

イソップ 仙台パルコ２店
Aesop Sendai PARCO2
Miyagi ／ 2016

トラフの小さな都市計画

TORAFU'S SMALL CITY PLANNING

DŌZO BENCH

NANYODO SHELF

Run Pit by au Smart Sports

WORLD CUP (YAMAGATA BIENNALE)

Garden in the Sky: Greenery and Delights

SHIBUYANORADIO

FREITAG Store Tokyo

FREITAG Store Tokyo Shibuya

SLIDING NATURE (Panasonic Milano Salone)

FROM THEORY TO PRACTICE WITH
ISHINOMAKI LABORATORY

DŌZO BENCH
2016

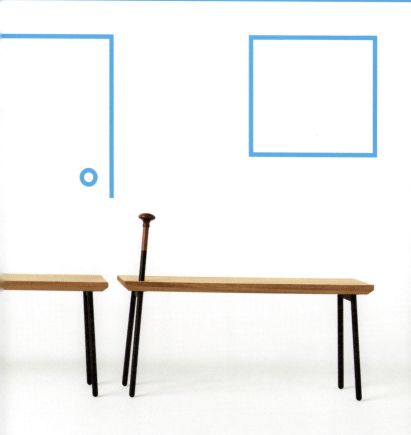

「どうぞ座ってください」と招き寄せるようなベンチの提案。個人の所有物でありながら、皆で共有できる家具を考えた。このベンチが各戸の軒先に並ぶことで、街の風景を変えていく。

This bench beckons passersby to sit down as if saying dōzo suwatte kudasai, which is Japanese for "Please, have a seat." We designed a piece of furniture that could be shared by all while remaining the private property of an individual. We sought to transform the city landscape with these outdoor benches to be placed in front of houses.

東京・神保町の建築専門書店、南洋堂の屋外に設置する本棚の計画。一般の人にも気軽に本を手に取ってもらえることと、毎日出し入れできる本棚が求められた。そこで、建物と共存するように、外壁の溝に板を差し込むだけの棚を提案した。本棚が街に溶け込み、行き交う人みんなのものとして共有しているような感覚を与えたいと考えた。

NANYODO SHELF
Tokyo／2011

We built a shelf on the exterior wall of Nanyodo, a bookstore specializing in books on architecture in Jimbocho, Tokyo. The project required a shelf that can be set up and removed easily while inspiring passers-by to pick up a book. Therefore, we proposed a shelf that would coexist with the building made of a single board inserted into the groove of the wall. By blending into the cityscape, this book shelf appears to belong to everyone.

皇居の周囲約5kmを走るランナーに向けた施設。パレスサイドビル内の一角に、ロッカースペース、シャワー設備、物販コーナーやラウンジスペースなどを併設する。仕事帰りの人が運動へとスムーズに切り替えられる場を象徴するように、湾曲した壁面によるトンネル状の空間を提案した。男女のスペースを分けるトンネルを抜けると、皇居周辺の緑豊かな風景が広がる。オフィスビル内部ですべてのことが完結しがちな現状に対して、外を感じ、街と繋がることのできる施設を提案した。小さな内装計画ではあるが、利用者にとって、街全体がランニングコースに描き換えられたかのように見えてくる。

This facility is geared to runners using the 5-km circuit around the Tokyo Imperial Palace. Located in a corner of the Palaceside Building, the facility offers locker rooms fitted with showers, a meeting lounge and a boutique as well. For those who wish to integrate exercise to their schedule after work-hours, we proposed a tunnel-like space made of sinuous walls. At the junction between the men's and women's areas, the tunnel presents a great view on the greening Imperial grounds. Although nowadays everything tends to be done inside office buildings, we proposed that the facility should link the inner and outer spaces. Small interior planning as it was, the facility allows the users to feel as if the city itself were redrawn as one big running track.

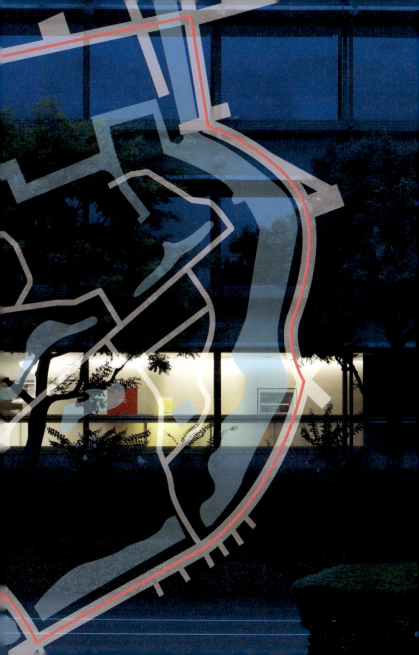

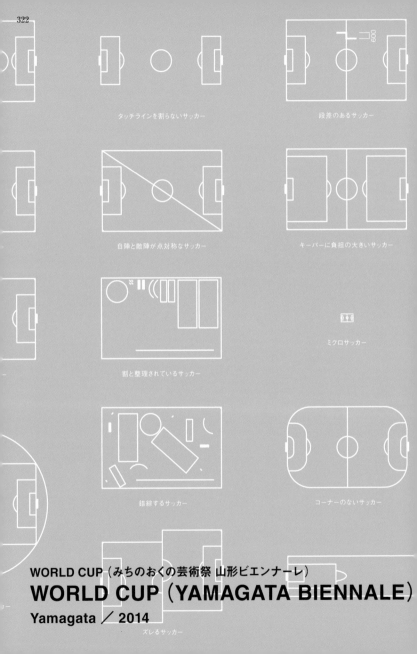

WORLD CUP（みちのおくの芸術祭 山形ビエンナーレ）
WORLD CUP (YAMAGATA BIENNALE)
Yamagata / 2014

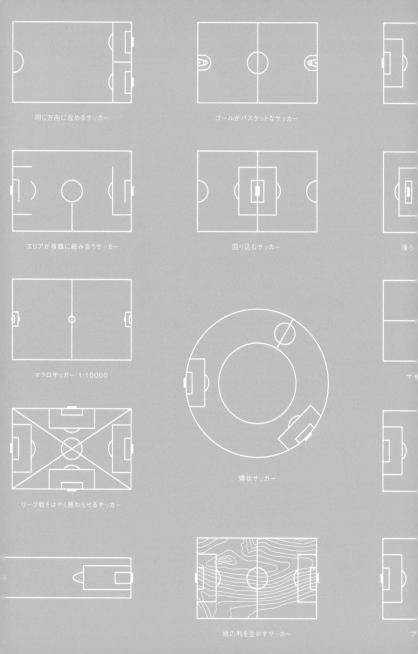

「みちのおくの芸術祭 山形ビエンナーレ 2014」において、スポーツを切り口にしたコミュニケーションアートとして、新しいサッカーコートを提案した。設計図で描く1本の線が人の行動を大きく左右するように、見慣れたサッカーコートの白線を少し変えることで、新しいコミュニケーションの場を創造する"スポーツ×建築"の実験。ドーナツ型のサッカーコートが、都市と人とを繋ぐ接点となる。

Using sport as an outlet for communication art, we presented a new type of soccer field during the 2014 Yamagata Biennale. Recognizing that the lines drawn on a diagram can greatly affect people's actions, we sought to create a new space that would foster communication by slightly reconfiguring the familiar white lines found on a soccer field through this experiment between *sports and architecture*. This donut-shaped soccer field became the point of contact between people and the city.

池袋駅に直結する西武池袋本店の屋上の改修計画。閑散としていた屋上を、都会に居ながら季節が感じられ、さまざまなフードを楽しめる場として再生する。印象派の風景画をモチーフに、屋上全体を水面に見立てて青色のタイルを敷き詰め、水面に浮かぶ蓮の葉をイメージした円形のデッキによって屋上空間に憩いの場をつくり出す。デッキの上のパラソルや円形の家具が層状に重なり、フラットな屋上に起伏をつくる。屋上という、非日常的で特別な場所の心地良さを感じながら、都市を俯瞰する新たな視点も感じることができる。

食と緑の空中庭園

Garden in the Sky: Greenery and Delights

Tokyo／2015

BEFORE

We renovated the roof of the Seibu Ikebukuro building directly linked to Ikebukuro Station. To do so, we repurposed the unused rooftop into a lively space where one can experience the seasons' offerings while enjoying different kinds of foods. Using impressionist landscapes as a motif, we carved out a place for relaxation and refreshment by covering the roof in blue tiles to give it the appearance of a body of water and fitted it with circular decks representing lotus leaves floating on the water surface. Each deck is fitted with round tables under a parasol and the layers of circular shapes create a relief on the otherwise flat roof. The rooftop garden offers an extraordinary feeling and a comfortable environment from where to experience a new vantage point on the city.

渋谷のラジオ
SHIBUYANORADIO
Tokyo ／ 2016

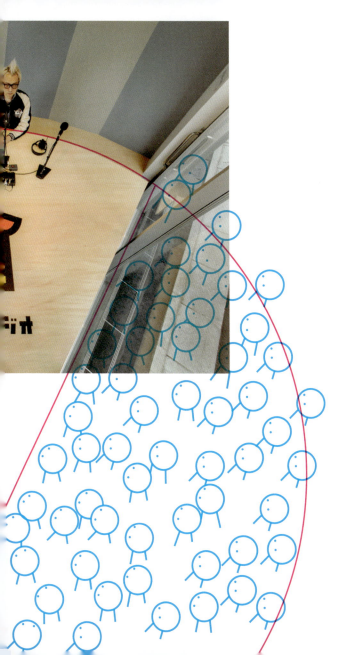

渋谷区全域を放送エリアとするコミュニティFM局「渋谷のラジオ」の放送スタジオ内装計画。同局はクリエイティブディレクター・箭内道彦氏が立ち上げ、地域コミュニティの可能性を広げることを目指す。渋谷駅周辺の再開発に伴い、駅から延びる新しい通り沿いの角地にある環境から、街に近い開放的なスタジオとした。ゲストは、中央の大きな扇形のテーブルを掘りごたつのように囲む。街へ広がる大きな円卓を思わせ、スタジオを取り巻く人びとも、このテーブルを共有して番組に参加しているような感覚になる。街との接点となるラジオ放送局の具現化を試みた。

隣の仮囲いがはずれると、新しい通りが現れ
外から取り囲むことができる。

Once the adjacent boarding is taken down,
it will reveal the new street which will frame the studio from outside.

We performed the interior design for the studio of "SHIBUYANORADIO", a community FM station broadcasting to all of Shibuya Ward. Helmed by creative director Michihiko Yanai, the station is intended to broaden the horizons of the local community. The studio is found along a new street that extends from the train station as part of an initiative to redevelop the area surrounding Shibuya Station and was setup to be an open studio in proximity to the city. Guests can sit in around a wide fan-shaped table like they would at a traditional low table over a recessed floor known as a hori-gotatsu that appears to extend into the street like a big round table, thus giving the impression that people surrounding the studio are sharing the same table and taking part in the program. We sought to create a radio station that would act as a point of contact with the city.

FREITAG Store Tokyo
Tokyo / 2011

使用済みのトラックの幌、自転車のチューブ、廃車のシートベルトを使った、メッセンジャーバッグやアクセサリーを展開するFREITAG（フライターグ）のアジア初の旗艦店。銀座の角地に建つ築50年のビルの1、2階が売り場になる。ストリートが起源のブランドの特性を踏まえて、街並みの延長にあるような店舗を目指した。ファサードの大型ガラスパネルをスライドさせると、店内と街路との境界がないオープンな場所となり、イベント時には店内の活気が街にあふれ出す。

内装仕上げ完了時の状態。既存躯体の表情を残すため、床を磨きパッチワーク状に補修して、補修範囲を最低限にとどめた。

A view of the completed interior. In order to reveal as much of the original character of the building, the existing floors were polished and mended while repairs were carried out in the most minimal possible way.

オープニングイベント時の店舗内外の様子。
A view of the store interior during the opening event.

FREITAG, a Swiss brand of messenger bags and accessories made out of recycled truck tarpaulins, bicycle air chambers and seat belts of disused cars, opened its first Asian flagship store in Tokyo. The store is located on a corner site in Ginza and occupies the first and second floors of a 50-year-old building. We had aimed for the store to be an extension of the street, of which the brand is characteristically originated from. In order to allow the liveliness of the surrounding streets to naturally enter into the store interior, the large glass panels making up the storefront can be fully slid opened.

FREITAG Store Tokyo Shibuya
Tokyo／2013

FREITAG 銀座店に続く、渋谷店の内外装計画。明治通りとキャットストリート、ふたつの通りに面する特殊な立地に、リペア工房を併設した店舗が求められた。店内を、ふたつの通りを繋ぐもうひとつの"ストリート"として捉え、人の流れを新しくつくり出せないかと考えた。中央に引かれた道路の延長のような白線と、街路灯の照明によってストリートの雰囲気を演出しながら、往来する人びとを自然に店内へと誘導する。ひとつの店舗でありながら、街中の人の流れに変化を与えている。

Following the Ginza location, we designed the interior of a FREITAG store in Shibuya. The site faces both Meiji Street in the front and Cat Street on the back side. We were asked to build a repair laboratory featuring this unique location. Therefore, by rethinking the flow of people, we imagined the store interior to be a side street connecting the two streets perpendicularly. White lines drawn on the middle of the floor suggest a road extending from outside, while street lamps create a street atmosphere that invites people naturally in to the store. This site not only works as a store, but also affects the flow of people walking in the street.

SLIDING NATURE (Panasonic Milano Salone)
Milano, Italy／2014

「ミラノサローネ」での、パナソニックの展示会場構成。襖や障子など、日本古来の建具の特徴を活かし、引き戸のみで構成した家型オブジェクトのインスタレーションを提案した。引き戸を開放すれば囲い込んでいた領域は消え去り、周囲の環境に同化する。扉というものの域を超えた、動く壁による空間で、ダイナミックに自然との新しい関係性を築いた。重厚な西洋建築を背景に、自動運転の真っ白な引き戸が中庭をゆっくりと横断する。壁に囲まれた"私"の空間が、開放されて"公"の場になる、という反復運動を通じて、都市へのまなざしを描き換える

We were invited to design the Panasonic exhibition site at the "Milano Salone." The key characteristic of this installation is a house-shaped structure featuring traditional Japanese fittings such as sliding doors, fusuma and shoji. As they open, the enclosing boundaries disappear and the inner space integrates with the surrounding environment. These moving walls function as more than doors by creating a space that defines a new, dynamic relationship with nature. The pure-white sliding doors offer an eye-catching sight against the massive Western architecture as they automatically slide away from the structure at the center of the courtyard. Moreover, the repeated transition from an enclosed *private* space to an open *public* one helps redefine our vision of the city.

石巻工房での実践

FROM THEORY TO PRACTICE WITH ISHINOMAKI LABORATORY

「石巻工房」は東日本大震災を機に、宮城県石巻市でデザイナーを中心に市民工房として設立され、世界初のDIYメーカーとして発展している。トラフはいくつかのプロダクトをデザインしながら、オフィスやショップのデザインの協働を通して継続的に参加している。単一素材によるシンプルな形状のプロダクトは、あり合わせの材料で作るまかない料理にちなんで、"まかない家具"とも呼んでいる。「石巻工房」での取り組みは、働く人たちの場をつくる、というかたちでも地方都市に変化をもたらす。小さな家具のデザインを通じて、都市での生活をどれだけ豊かに変えることができるのか、「小さな都市計画」の実践的な試みを続けている。

Following the Great East Japan Earthquake, Ishinomaki Laboratory has evolved from a community workshop mainly geared towards designers into the world's first DIY manufacturer since its establishment in Ishinomaki City, Miyagi Prefecture. Torafu has designed several products and continues to collaborate with the furniture maker through the design of offices and shops. Named after makanai ryouri, which is a meal prepared for staff that makes use of nearby ingredients, we use the term makanai furniture to describe the simple form of products made with a single material. The efforts of Ishinomaki Laboratory even bring change to regional cities and towns by creating spaces for working people. They continuously experiment with how they can enrich city life through designing small pieces of furniture.

❶石巻工房は、震災後の復旧・復興のために自由に使える公共的な施設としてスタートした。❷❸初期のワークショップのひとつは仮設住宅の軒先の縁台製作だった。❹DIYのワークショップを通じて、被災者自らが手を動かす、新たなかたちの復興を目指す。❺工房長は元寿司職人の千葉隆博氏が務める。❻最初に移転した工房の壁面は、「ガリバーテーブル」の天板を再利用したもの。当時は小さかった工房も、移転して大きな規模となった。

❶ Ishinomaki Laboratory started out as a public establishment to be used freely for restoration and reconstruction initiatives after the Great East Japan Earthquake.
❷❸ One of the initial workshops involved the production of outdoor benches to be placed in front of temporary houses.
❹ The aim was to develop a new type of reconstruction by having disaster victims get directly involved through DIY workshops.
❺ The workshop leader is Takahiro Chiba, a former sushi chef.
❻ The "Gulliver Table" tabletop was the first wall surface to go up for the workshop after its relocation. The relocation also led the then-small laboratory to increase in size.

スカイデッキ
SKYDECK
2012

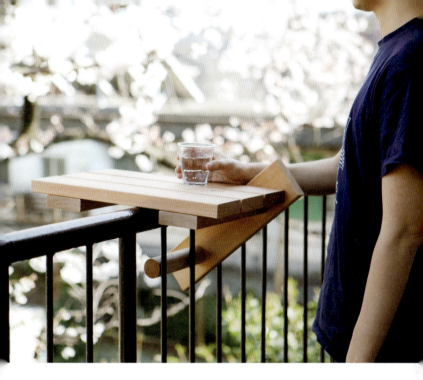

テラスを"敷地"に見立てて発想した、手すりに引っかけるだけの小さなテーブル。洗濯物を干している間に携帯やラジオを置いたり、気持ちの良い日にはテラスでビールを飲むためのカウンターにもなる。空中に浮かぶ「スカイデッキ」は、自宅のテラスを少しだけ都市に拡張する。

This is a small table that hooks onto a handrail, using a minimum number of pieces. You can put your mobile phone or a radio on it while you hang your laundry, or it can be used as a counter for having a beer on your balcony on a nice day. By imagining one's small balcony as a *site* floating in mid-air, the "SKYDECK" stretches the available space out by just a little bit—into the city beyond.

AA スツール
AA STOOL
2012

26 x 87mmの製材された1本のデッキ材からちょうど1脚ができる、シンプルなスツール。脚の部材の両端を少しだけ斜めにカットして組み合わせることで、座面を互いに支えあって自立する。組み合わされたスツールはふたつに分けられ、来客があった時や、小さなスペースでは単体としても使える。スツール同士を前後に重ねて複数スタッキングすると、ベンチにもなる。横から見るとアルファベットの"A"に見えるこのスツールは、街中でも小さなコミュニティの場をつくり出す。

This is a simple stool made of 26mm by 87mm dimensional lumber, where the legs are cut at a slightly diagonal angle at both ends. Combining these leg pieces together allows the stool to stand, and at the same time provides support for the seat of the stool. A set is composed of two stools, which can be integrated together into one unit. It can be separated into individual stools as required; to be used by visitors or within small spaces. From the side, the stool looks like the letter 'A'. By stacking and lining up the stools, a bench can be created, acting as a small, on-the-go gathering spot for the community.

Rapha Mobile Cycle Club
2015

サイクリングウェアブランド Rapha の
移動式販売とサイクリストのライドハブとなる什器と車両のデザイン。
車両周囲にコミュニティの場をつくり出す。

We designed the fixtures and vehicle to be used for mobile sales,
as well as a cyclist rest stop for the cycling clothing maker, Rapha,
to create a community space around the vehicle.

trees for everyone by Android
Tokyo／2015

六本木ヒルズアリーナで開催された
Android搭載スマートフォンによるイルミネーションの計画。
「AAスツール」を組み上げた12本のツリーが場を演出する。

We designed this illumination display, which was made using
Android-operating devices, for an event held at the Roppongi Hills Arena.
The site features 12 "AA STOOLs" stacked into the shape of a tree.

3.11以後の建築／
トラフ建築設計事務所＋石巻工房
Architecture since 3.11/
TORAFU ARCHITECTS +
ISHINOMAKI LABORATORY
Ishikawa／2014

金沢21世紀美術館で行われた展覧会での展示計画。
高さ3.6mに巨大化した「AAスツール」をシンボルに
その構造体の下では「石巻工房」のドキュメンタリー映像を鑑賞できる。

This is a design for an exhibition held
at the 21st Century Museum of Contemporary Art, Kanazawa.
Here, visitors can enjoy screenings of a documentary
featuring Ishinomaki Laboratory,
while sitting under a symbolic structure
made from 3.6m high oversized "AA STOOLs".

移転して大きくなった現在の石巻工房。
A view of the new and bigger Ishinomaki Laboratory following its relocation.

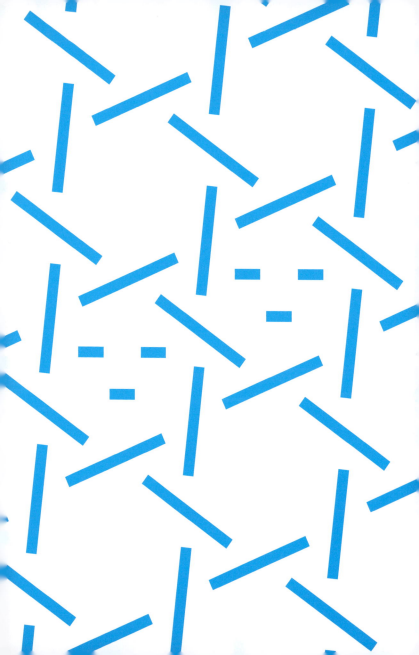

こころの隙間に、
知らぬまに建築を建ててしまうふたり

原 研哉

気づいたら、こころのわずかの隙間に建築が建てられている。トラフの鈴野浩一と禿 真哉は今までは敷地とは思われなかった意外性のある場所に建築を生み出す才能を持った建築家である。油断していると、ふたつ、みっつ、とこころの内にトラフの建築を携えてしまっている。

鈴野浩一も禿真哉も、誤解を恐れずにいうなら、威圧感のないタイプで、緊張感を四方に張り巡らせている従来の建築家とは佇まいの違う人たちである。この雰囲気はスタッフにまで浸透していて、打ち合わせの際には、実にほのぼのとなごやかな雰囲気になる。なじみやすい空気感で、一緒にいる人たちの懐にすっと入り込む。そうしようと努めても実現できる技ではない。独特のひとあたりのよさと、どんなに無理なことでも相談できそうな安心感が、トラフという建築家ユニットの素地であるように思われる。

トラフを世に送り出した作品の一つに「空気の器」というものがある。これは紙に、極めて細やかな切れ目を稠密に配していくという方法で設計されたものである。七夕飾りにも似たような方法が見られるが、「空気の器」はそれを徹底的に微細・精密に行うことで、紙はまるで深い壺のような奥行きを持った器として伸展していくのである。紙の表裏にヴィヴィッドな対比を生み出す色彩を配すると、立体に立ち上がった際に表裏の色が微細なスリットからのぞきあうことで干渉しあい、めく

るめく色彩現象が立ち上がるのである。
建築の構造というのは、建築物の大きさによって変化するわけだが、手のひらの上に立ち上がるほどのものであれば、紙の繊維は十分に強靭で、「空気の器」はいかにも弱そうに見えながらも弾性に富んでいて破綻がない。だからこれに触れる人々は皆、紙がこんなにも柔軟に伸展し、まさに空気をはらんだ器のように見えるその風情に魅了されるのである。なんのために用いるのかわからない「空気の器」であるが、人々はこれをたしかに建築家の仕事と受けとめ、そこに新時代の建築の空気を感じ取ったであろう。

僕が二つ目にトラフの仕事に瞠目したのは「コロロデスク」という、家具のような、最小の部屋のような建築である。現代の人々は、知らぬ間に目に見えない個室に住み始めていたのかもしれない。通信技術の進歩によって、人々はいつも誰かと繋がろうとしている。同じ屋根の下に住んでいる家族だけではなく、多元的に他者と繋がっている。そういうタイミングで登場した「コロロデスク」は、化粧板メーカーの仕事らしく、色もきれいで可愛いものであったが、一方では「個」に分断され始めている現代人の暮らしを端的に具体化するものとして、とても生々しく心に刺さった。そして、こういうものを無意識に欲していた、自分自身のあり方をも、そこに見るような気がしたのである。自分一人のための、自分のこころを収納す

る空間を、みんな欲しがっている。それを、実に可愛らしく、やさしく、そして的確に建築化した仕事である。

また、トラフは「犬のための建築」展においては「ワンモック」というオブジェクトを提案している。これは、飼い主の匂いを好み、その衣類の上に寝たがるという犬の習性に着目した、犬と飼い主のための新しい空間提案である。簡単な木のフレームに飼い主のセーター、あるいはTシャツをかぶせると、ハンモックのようなやわらかい空中浮遊の寝床が出来上がる。犬は大好きな飼い主の匂いの上で、心地よく安らぐことができる、という着想である。人類とともに生きることを宿命づけられた犬に、「現代の暮らしの文脈の中でどんな建築が構想できるか」という問いに対するトラフらしい回答である。この展覧会の企画者として、図面さえあれば、飼い主が日曜大工でできるような単純明快なものを、と考えていたのであるが、トラフの回答は、ほぼ的の真ん中を射抜くものであった。「犬」と聞いただけで眉根を寄せてしまう建築家もいるし、建築というのはもっと深遠なテーマに向き合うべきであると考える向きもあるだろうが、「犬のための建築」と聞いて、そんなものが設計できる機会があるならと、嬉々としてそこに向き合おうとするトラフのような建築家こそ、人の心理の中に、新たな建築の敷地を発見できるのではないだろうか。

時々、SNSを介した彼らの発信するメッセージを眺めている。考えてみると、彼らほどSNSを上手に使う建築家はいない。つぶやくように、独り言のように発せられる素朴な、そして心配りの利いた言葉と、人の心の隙間に建てられるような不思議な建築を反芻するにつけ、これまでとは違った意味での「新たな空間」の到来を感じている。

資本主義も末期にさしかかっており、日本の少子高齢化社会の問題を持ち出すまでもなく、僕らは新たな時代の潮流に向き合っていくことになる。潮の流れが正反対からやってくるときも、風を利用しながらジグザグに、それでも前に進んでいくヨットのように、僕らはゆっくりとしたたかに、柔軟かつタフに、前へと進んでいかなくてはならない。そんな時代の建築家として、トラフの二人の存在が、光を放って見えるのである。

Two men building architecture that finds its way into your heart

Kenya Hara

Before I knew it, I realized that there was architecture standing inside a small space inside my heart. Koichi Suzuno and Shinya Kamuro from TORAFU are architects who have the ability to build architecture in unusual locations that one would not have considered to be a suitable site up until then. Before you know it, you would find two or three TORAFU architectural pieces within your heart. If I may say so, Koichi Suzuno and Shinya Kamuro are not the kind of high pressure conventional architects that emanate tension in every direction. This relaxed atmosphere extends to the staff; meetings are actually carried out in a warm and friendly atmosphere. They quickly enter the heart of other people with this smooth attitude. This is not something that can be accomplished through effort alone. I believe that the framework for TORAFU ARCHITECTS revolves around the individual quality of each person involved and the sense of reassurance they provide by accepting consultations for any kind of job, even those that seem impossible.

One of the pieces that put TORAFU into the spotlight was "airvase". The design method called for paper with extremely fine gaps arranged throughout. This method seems similar to one used for Tanabata decorations, but by using a delicate and fine process elaborated for "airvase", the paper develops into a container with a sense of depth such as that of a deep vessel. By arranging colors to add vivid contrast to each side of the paper, the colors peek out through the fine slits and interfere with each other when the piece is stood

up as a three-dimensional object. This phenomenon creates a dazzling color effect.
In architecture, the structure of construction changes depending on the size of the building, but when it comes to something that can stand on the palm of your hand, the paper fibers are sufficiently robust; "airvase" may look weak but the high degree of elasticity means it will not break. People who come into contact with it are charmed by its elegance due to its great flexibility and appearance that resembles a container swelling with air. "airvase" may have no clear purpose, but people identify it as the work of architects. Perhaps they perceive it as part of a new age of architecture.

The second TORAFU piece that caught my eye was the "koloro-desk", which is architecture that resembles something between furniture and a tiny room. People today have probably been living in a kind of invisible private room without realizing it. Thanks to advances in communication technology, people are always connected to others. Not only are they connected to family living under the same roof, but also to a multitude of other people. The "koloro-desk", whose timely appearance was apparently requested by a decorative plywood manufacturer, might have pretty colors and a cute look, but it's the way in which it directly gives shape to the personal space of modern people's lives that struck me in a refreshing way. I also felt like it allowed me to see my own situation in the way that I subconsciously desired such a thing. Everyone wants a kind of space that is very personal, in which they can store their emotions. This is a lovely, sweet, and precise architectural realization of such a concept.

TORAFU also displayed an object called "wanmock" at the Architecture for Dogs exhibition. This is a new space proposal for the sake of dogs and their owners that recognizes the way in which dogs prefer the scent of their owner and have a tendency to sleep on top of their owner's clothes. The owner's sweater or t-shirt is placed on a simple wooden frame to create a soft bed in midair that acts like a hammock. The idea was to have the dog be able to relax on top of his favorite master's scent. This was TORAFU's answer to the question "What kind of architecture can you conceive within the context of modern day living?" in regard to dogs to who are bound by fate to live together with humans. As an organizer of this exhibition, we were thinking that it would be good to have something that a pet owner could put together easily by themselves with a clear blueprint in hand, but TORAFU's answer hit the target just about in the middle. Some architects would frown at the mere mention of a *dog*, thinking that architecture should be used for more serious themes, but it is precisely architects like TORAFU, who gladly accepted the opportunity to design Architecture for Dogs, that will discover new architectural spaces within the human mind.

I sometimes browse the messages they leave on social networking sites. When

I think about it, no other architects use social media as skillfully as they do. By their simple and thoughtful words as well as architecture that mysteriously finds its way into your heart, I feel the coming of a *new space* that is different from what came before.

We are facing the tide of a new age as the era of capitalism draws to an end and Japan grapples with demographic problems such as a low birthrate and aging population. Sometimes the tide comes from the opposite direction, but like a yacht moving forward while zigzagging with the wind, we also must slowly but steadily move forward while remaining flexible and strong. Living in such an age, the existence of the TORAFU unit is like a beacon of light.

作品データ Data on works

1: principal use
2: collaborator
3: constructor
4: producer
5: material
6: size
7: location
8: site area
9: total floor area
10: number of stories
11: structure
12: design period
13: construction period
14: term

TEMPLATE IN CLASKA
1: monthly hotel
2: lighting design: MAXRAY
3: IKEYA
7: Hotel CLASKA, Meguro, Tokyo
9: 18 ㎡ x3 rooms
12: 2004.02-03
13: 2004.04

NIKE 1LOVE
1: shop
2: lighting design: On&Off
3: ISHIMARU, MIHOYA GLASS
7: Shibuya, Tokyo
9: 108 ㎡
12: 2006.11-12
13: 2006.12-2007.01

HOUSE IN KOHOKU
1: house
2: structural design: MID architectural structure laboratory/furniture design: TAIJI FUJIMORI ATELIER/fabric design: NUNO/lighting design: spangle
3: YAMASHO
7: Yokohama, Kanagawa
8: 230.8 ㎡
9: 67.4 ㎡
10: 1F+loft
11: RC
12: 2007.01-11
13: 2007.12-2008.07

AKQA Tokyo Office
1: office
2: lighting design: Izumi Okayasu Lighting Design/furniture: E&Y, gleam/plants: SOLSO
3: AMANO, ISHIMARU
7: Shibuya, Tokyo
9: 709.2 ㎡
12: 2014.08-11
13: 2014.11-2015.01

gold wedding ring
1: product
4: gallery deux poissons
5: gold (k18 yellow gold), silver plating
12: 2012.01-02

dollhouse chair
1: product
2: design: TORAFU ARCHITECTS (Koichi Suzuno, Alicja Strzyżyńska)/styling: Fumiko Sakuhara
4: ICHIRO
5: white birch plywood
6: dollhouse: W710xD185xH540 mm/chair: W365xD355xH540 mm, SH360 mm
12: 2014.09-10

airvase
1: product
2: package design: TAKAIYAMA
4: KAMI NO KOUSAKUJO
12: 2009.10-12
13: 2009.12-2010.01

Light Loom (Canon Milano Salone)
1: exhibition site
2: producer: TRUNK/supervisor: ZITOMORI/visual design: WOW
3: Taiyo Kogyo
7: Superstudio Più ART POINT, Tortona, Milano, Italy
9: 825 ㎡
12: 2010.09-2011.03
13: 2011.04.01-10
14: 2011.04.12-17

Gulliver Table
1: exhibition site
2: structural design: Ohno JAPAN
3: ISHIMARU
6: W2,400xD51,600xH400-2,150 mm
7: Tokyo Midtown DESIGN TOUCH Park, Minato, Tokyo
12: 2011.07-10
13: 2011.10.24-26
14: 2011.10.28-11.06

CMYK
1: product
3: SFIDA
12: 2008.07-10
13: 2008.10-12

koloro-desk / koloro-stool
1: product
2: production collaboration: INOUE INDUSTRIES
4: ICHIRO
5: koloro-desk: polyester plywood (base material: lauan plywood), Japanese ash/koloro-stool: lauan plywood, Japanese ash, fabric
6: koloro-desk: W736xD556xH1,318 mm, TH700 mm/koloro-stool: SH430mm, SH530 mm
12: 2011.02-2012.02

HOUSE IN MEGUROHONCHO
1: house
2: structural design: Ohno JAPAN/lighting design: MAXRAY
3: TSUKI-ZO
7: Meguro, Tokyo
8: 109.7 ㎡
9: 123.7 ㎡
10: 3F+BF
11: RC
12: 2011.03-07
13: 2011.08-12

HOUSE IN OOKAYAMA
1: house
2: structural design: Ohno JAPAN/fabric design: NUNO/lighting design: MAXRA
3: AO
7: Meguro, Tokyo
8: 76.16 ㎡
9: 104.5 ㎡
10: 3F+storage
11: wood

12: 2009.11-2010.06
13: 2010.06-11

Big T
1: house
2: design collaboration: Hisashi Hojin
9: 1,369.91 ㎡
12: 2015.08-2016.08
13: 2015.11-2016.08

TORAFU's Haunted house is a "Haunted play house" (MUSEUM OF CONTEMPORARY ART TOKYO)
1: exhibition site
2: lighting design: ENDO-Lighting
3: ISHIMARU
7: MUSEUM OF CONTEMPORARY ART TOKYO "GHOSTS, UNDERPANTS and STARS", Koto, Tokyo
9: haunted house: 173.9 ㎡ /bridge with eyes: 87.2 ㎡
12: 2012.10-2013.06
13: 2013.06.20-27
14: 2013.06.29-09.08

wanmock
1: product
2: direction: KENYA HARA + HARA DESIGN INSTITUTE, Nippon Design Center
4: INOUE INDUSTRIES
5: plywood, t15mm
6: W546xD731xH398 mm
12: 2012.06-08

"ZERO HOUR" TOKYO ROSE'S LAST TAPE
1: stage set
2: writer stage, director, set design: Miwa Yanagi/sound design: Formant Brothers/cast: Yohei Matsukdo, Hinako Arao, Keisuke Yoshida, Norie Takahashi, Maki Takahashi, Sayaka Oda, Aki
3: KANAGAWA ARTS THEATRE, AICHI PREFECTURAL ART THEATER
12: 2013.04-06
13: 2013.06-07
14: KANAGAWA ARTS THEATRE 2013.07.12-15, AICHI PREFECTURAL ART THEATER 2013.08.30-09.01

MOTOMI KAWAKAMI CHRONICLE 1966-2011
1: exhibition site
2: supervisor: Motomi Kawakami/producer: TRUNK/graphic design: TAKAIYAMA
3: TOKYO STUDIO
7: Living Design Center OZONE 3F park tower hall, Shinjuku, Tokyo
9: 443 ㎡
12: 2011.05-09
13: 2011.09
14: 2011.09.09-25

Catch-bowl
1: product
4: TANSEISHA
5: bent plywood, sycamore, stainless steel, magnet
6: Φ400 mm
12: 2011.04-06

clopen
1: product
4: TANSEISHA
5: aluminum, Japanese ash, magnet
6: W900xD150xH34 mm
12: 2012.04-06

cobrina
1: product
4: HIDA SANGYO
5: oak
12: 2012.12-2013.07

tapehook
1: product
2: package design: TAKAIYAMA/accessories: gallery deux poissons
4: KAMI NO KOUSAKUJO
5: paper
6: W15xD17xH45 mm
12: 2010.12-2011.02
14: 2011.04.27-05.22

Y150 NISSAN PAVILION
1: exhibition site
2: produce: TBWA＼HAKUHODO /planning: HAKUHODO
3: MURAYAMA

7: Yokohama, Kanagawa
9: 2,196 ㎡
12: 2008.09-2009.02
13: 2009.03-04
14: 2009.04.28-09.27

NIKE JMC
1: office, exhibition space
2: project management: PAE Design and Facility Management/lighting design: ENDO-Lighting/2F auditorium lighting design: Hyper Active Studio/sign design: TAKAIYAMA/art work: Takeshi Abe
3: TOA, ISHIMARU, E&Y, ITOKI MARKET SPACE
7: Tokyo Bayside area
9: 5,684.8 ㎡
10: 6F
11: SRC
12: 2008.12-2009.07
13: 2009.07-09

LIGHT LIGHT DESK
1: product
4: GLAESER WOGG AG
5: aluminum composite panel, linoleum, LED panel
6: W688xD533xH1,078 mm
12: 2015.02

minä perhonen koti
1: shop
2: lighting design: MAXRAY
3: TOKYO STUDIO, Nakamura paint, E&Y, NOMURA
7: Kanagawa Shonan T-SITE, Fujisawa, Kanagawa
9: 66.8 ㎡
12: 2014.06-2015.02
13: 2014.08-11, 2015.03

water balloon
1: product
2: lighting design: MAXRAY
4: Garasukikakusya
5: glass, fluorescent recycled glass, LED
6: W80xD80xH217 mm
12: 2013.06-09
13: 2013.09-11

Aesop Shin-Marunouchi
1: shop
2: graphics: Aesop
3: ISHIMARU
7: Shin-Marunouchi Building, Marunouchi, Chiyoda, Tokyo
9: 22.5 ㎡
12: 2012.02-06
13: 2012.06

Aesop Yokohama Bay Quarter
1: shop
2: graphics: Aesop
3: ISHIMARU
7: Yokohama Bay Quarter ANNEX, Yokohama, Kanagawa
9: 23.2 ㎡
12: 2012.02-06
13: 2012.06

Aesop Shibuya
1: shop
2: lighting design: ENDO-Lighting/graphics: Aesop
3: ISHIMARU
7: Shibuya, Tokyo
9: 22.6 ㎡
12: 2012.12-2013.03
13: 2013.01-03

Aesop Kawaramachi
1: shop
2: lighting design: ENDO-Lighting, MAXRAY/graphics: Aesop
3: &S
8: Kawaramachi, Kyoto
9: 86 ㎡
12: 2013.09-11
13: 2013.11-12

Aesop Grand Front Osaka
1: shop
2: lighting design: MAXRAY/graphics: Aesop
3: &S
7: GRAND FRONT OSAKA, Kita, Osaka
9: 47.4 ㎡
12: 2014.01-05
13: 2014.04-05

Aesop Midtown
1: shop
2: lighting design: DAIKO/graphics: Aesop
3: &S
7: Tokyo Midtown, Minato, Tokyo
9: 24 ㎡
12: 2014.12-2015.03
13: 2015.02-03

Aesop NEWoMan Shinjuku
1: shop
2: lighting design: DAIKO/graphics: Aesop
3: &S
7: NEWoMan Shinjuku, Shinjuku, Tokyo
9: 45.6 ㎡
12: 2015.04-12
13: 2015.12-2016.01

Aesop Sendai PARCO2
1: shop
2: lighting design: DAIKO/graphics: Aesop
3: &S
7: Aesop Sendai Parco 2, Sendai, Miyagi
9: 48 ㎡
12: 2015.09-2016.03
13: 2016.04-05

DŌZO BENCH
1: product (prototype)
4: TANSEISHA
5: red cedar, steel, ready-made cane
6: W1,000xD235xH720mm, SH450mm
12: 2016.04-06

NANYODO SHELF
1: product
3: TORAFU ARCHITECTS
7: Book shop NANYODO, Chiyoda, Tokyo
12: 2011.07-08

Run Pit by au Smart Sports
1: facility space
2: producer: Hakuhodo Experience Design/project management: FCI Design and Management/lighting design: On&Off/sign & color design: TAKAIYAMA/fabric design: NUNO/furniture: Interoffice
3: TAKENAKA, ISHIMARU
7: PALACESIDE BUILDING, Chiyoda, Tokyo
9: 217.8 ㎡
12: 2010.02-05
13: 2010.05-06

WORLD CUP (YAMAGATA BIENNALE)
1: exhibition site
2: graphics: akaoni Design/bib's design: STORE
3: TOKYO STUDIO, TIMBER COURT
7: Bunshyokan, Hatago, Yamagata
9: 240 ㎡
12: 2013.01-2014.09
13: 2014.09
14: 2014.09.20-10.19

Garden in the Sky: Greenery and Delights
1: roof garden
2: total direction & sign design: Masaski Hiromura (Hiromura Design Office)/collaboration planning: EARTHSCAPE/lighting design: LIGHTDESIGN/plants: Hibiya Amenis/furniture: TISTOU
7: SEIBU IKEBUKURO 9F, Toshima, Tokyo
9: roof garden: 4,974 ㎡ /loft: 173.6 ㎡
12: 2014.08-12
13: 2015.01-04

SHIBUYANORADIO
1: broadcast studio
2: management: NPO CQ/character design: Bunpei Yorifuji
3: ISHIMARU, KLASSE
7: Shibuya, Tokyo
9: 46.3 ㎡
12: 2015.07-2016.01
13: 2016.01-02

FREITAG Store Tokyo
1: shop
2: sign & graphic design: FREITAG/lighting design: Naito Denkyo
3: ISHIMARU
7: Chuo, Tokyo
9: 75.8 ㎡

12: 2011.05-10
13: 2011.09-10

FREITAG Store Tokyo Shibuya
1: shop
2: sign graphic: FREITAG/lighting design: ENDO-Lighting/supervisor: spillmann echsle architekten ag
3: ISHIMARU
7: Shibuya, Tokyo
9: 122.8 ㎡
12: 2013.04-08

SLIDING NATURE
(Panasonic Milano Salone)
1: exhibition site
2: planning: R+W/lighting design: Izumi Okayasu Lighting Design/sound-lighting technical: LUFTZUG/graphic design: TAKAIYAMA
3: Dott. Arch, XILOGRAFIA NUOVA SRL
7: Milano University, Milano, Italy
9: 1,400 ㎡
12: 2013.10-2014.03
13: 2014.04-05
14: 2014.04.08-13

SKYDECK
1: product
3: ISHINOMAKI LABORATORY
5: Canadian red cedar
6: W308xD453xH90mm (when folded) 450mm (when set up)
12: 2010.09-2012.02

AA STOOL
1: product
3: ISHINOMAKI LABORATORY
5: Canadian red cedar
6: W328xD422(330 for each separated stool)xH560 mm
12: 2012.09-10

rapha Mobile Cycle Club
1: moving stall
2: furniture: ISHINOMAKI LABORATORY
3: E&Y
12: 2015.08-10
13: 2015.10

trees for everyone by Android
1: exhibition site
2: plan, whole produce & progress management: DENTSU, Dentsu isobar/event produce & progress management: DENTSU TEC/program & technical direction: BIRDMAN/movie: Kouichiro Tsujikawa (GLASSLOFT), MONSTER, KOKIHIFUMI, Tokyo Sound Production, BEPOP, Liberty House, moi, TACS ODAIBA STUDIO, TYO Productions1, Fantasista, Freelance/furniture production: ISHINOMAKI LABORATORY/design, graphic: TAKI corporation/music: CORNELIUS, aiin
3: ISHINOMAKI LABORATORY
7: ROPPONGI HILLS ARENA, Minato, Tokyo
9: 1,120.0 ㎡
12: 2015.11-12
13: 2015.11.16-12.14
14: 2015.12.14-16

Architecture since 3.11 / TORAFU ARCHITECTS + ISHINOMAKI LABORATORY
1: exhibition site
3: ISHINOMAKI LABORATORY
7: 21st Century Museum of Contemporary Art, Kanazawa, Ishikawa
12: 2014.06-09
13: 2014.01
14: 2014.11.1-2015.05.10

トラフ建築設計事務所

鈴野浩一(すずの こういち)と禿 真哉(かむろ しんや)により2004年に設立。建築の設計をはじめ、インテリアデザイン、展覧会の会場構成、プロダクト、空間インスタレーションなど多岐にわたり、建築的な思考をベースに取り組んでいる。主な作品に「テンプレート イン クラスカ」、「港北の住宅」、「空気の器」、「ガリバーテーブル」、「Big T」など。2011年「光の織機(Canon Milano Salone)」でエリータデザインアワード最優秀賞受賞。2015年「空気の器」がモントリオール美術館の永久コレクションに認定。『空気の器の本』、作品集『TORAFU ARCHITECTS 2004-2011 トラフ建築設計事務所のアイデアとプロセス』(共に美術出版社/2011年)、絵本『トラフの小さな都市計画』(平凡社/2012年)を刊行。(www.torafu.com)

STAFF

鈴野浩一 / Koichi Suzuno
禿 真哉 / Shinya Kamuro

草薙岳仁 / Takehito Kusanagi
Miska Kuntsi
坂根みなほ / Minaho Sakane
Adrian Steckeweh
勢井彩華 / Ayaka Sei
塚本 薫 / Kaoru Tsukamoto
辻尾一平 / Ippei Tsujio
森田夏子 / Natsuko Morita

2016年10月現在
as of Oct. 2016

PAST STAFF

浅田麻里 / Mari Asada
飴野りつ子 / Ritsuko Ameno
有原寿典 / Kazunori Arihara
飯塚之通 / Hisamichi Iizuka
五十嵐瑠衣 / Rui Igarashi
大塚安矢 / Aya Otsuka
朔 永吉 / Eikichi Saku
鈴木智仁 / Tomohito Suzuki
Alicja Strzyżyńska
田代朋彦 / Tomohiko Tashiro
魏 婷 / Wei Ting
中村尚弘 / Naohiro Nakamura
難波真史 / Naofumi Namba
宮井裕穂 / Yuho Miyai
村上里砂 / Risa Murakami
室岡 優 / Yu Murooka
山口英恵 / Hanae Yamaguchi
山家 明 / Akira Yamage
Jody Wong

TORAFU ARCHITECTS

Founded in 2004 by Koichi Suzuno and Shinya Kamuro, TORAFU ARCHITECTS employs a working approach based on architectural thinking. Works by the duo include a diverse range of products, from architectural design to interior design, exhibition space design, product design and spatial installations. Amongst some of their mains works are "TEMPLATE IN CLASKA", "HOUSE IN KOHOKU", "airvase", "Gulliver Table" and "Big T". In 2011, "Light Loom (Canon Milano Salone)" was awarded the Grand Prize of the Elita Design Award. In 2015, "airvase" become part of the permanent collection of Montreal Museum of Fine Arts. Published in 2011 were the *airvase book* and *TORAFU ARCHITECTS 2004-2011 Idea + Process* (by BIJUTSU SHUPPAN-SHA CO., LTD.) and in 2012, a picture book titled *TORAFU's Small City Planning* (by Heibonsha Limited). (www.torafu.com)

Koichi Suzuno

1973: Born in Kanagawa Prefecture
1996: Graduated from Department of Architecture, Science University of Tokyo
1998: Completed the Master Course of Architecture, Yokohama National University
1998-2001: Worked at Coelacanth K&H
2002-2003: Worked at Kerstin Thompson Architects / Melbourne
2004-: Founded TORAFU ARCHITECTS with Shinya Kamuro
2010-: Lecturer at Musashino Art University
2012-: Lecturer at Tama Art University
2014-: Guest professor at Kyoto Seika University

Shinya Kamuro

1974: Born in Shimane Prefecture
1997: Graduated from Department of Architecture, School of Science & Technology, Meiji University
1999: Completed the Master Course of Architecture, Meiji University
2000-2003: Worked at Jun Aoki & Associates
2004-: Founded TORAFU ARCHITECTS with Koichi Suzuno

鈴野浩一（すずの こういち）

1973年：神奈川県生まれ
1996年：東京理科大学工学部建築学科卒業
1998年：横浜国立大学大学院工学部建築学専攻修士課程修了
1998〜2001年：シーラカンスK&H勤務
2002〜2003年：Kerstin Thompson Architects（メルボルン）勤務
2004年〜：トラフ建築設計事務所共同主宰
2010年〜：武蔵野美術大学非常勤講師
2012年〜：多摩美術大学非常勤講師
2014年〜：京都精華大学客員教授

禿 真哉（かむろ しんや）

1974年：島根県生まれ
1997年：明治大学理工学部建築学科卒業
1999年：同大学大学院修士課程修了
2000〜2003年：青木淳建築計画事務所勤務
2004年〜：トラフ建築設計事務所共同主宰

クレジット Credits

英訳 English translation
川又勝利 Katsutoshi Kawamata
フランシスコ・ガルシア Francisco Garcia
ダニエル・マッキー Daniel Mackey

写真提供 Photographs
Paul Barbera / Where They Create
inside front cover, pp. 2-3, pp.11-12,
p. 20, pp. 22-23, p. 25, pp. 396-397,
pp. 404-409, pp. 411-414, p. 416,
inside back cover

新建築社 Shinkenchiku-sha
pp. 28-29, p. 32

阿野太一 Daici Ano
pp. 30-31, pp. 36-41, pp. 43-45,
p. 49, pp. 54-61, pp. 66-75, pp.
144-147, p. 151, pp. 154-155,
pp. 158-159, pp. 165-167, pp. 170-175,
pp. 178-183, pp. 188-193, p. 256,
p. 257 top, pp. 258-263, p. 266,
pp. 312-319, pp. 336-341, pp. 346-349,
pp. 351-353

皆川 聡 Satoshi Minakawa
p. 33

小川真輝 Masaki Ogawa
pp. 78-79, pp. 82-83, pp. 250-251,
pp. 278-281, pp. 306-307, pp. 370-371

田村孝介 Kosuke Tamura
p. 81

伊藤彰浩 Akihiro Ito
pp. 84-89, pp. 134-135, pp. 138-142

安永ケンタウロス Kentauros Yasunaga
pp. 92-93

冨田里美 Satomi Tomita
pp. 94-95, pp. 101-103

大木大輔 Daisuke Ohki
pp. 104-105, pp. 108-109,
pp. 114-115, pp. 224-229

下川大輔 Daisuke Shimokawa
pp. 106-107

吉次史成 Fuminari Yoshitsugu
pp. 118-127, pp. 196-197, pp. 200-203,
pp. 206-207, pp. 242-245, pp.254-255,
pp. 308-311, pp. 330-335, pp. 366-368,
pp. 372-373

太田拓実 Takumi Ota
pp. 130-131, pp. 272-275,
pp. 282-299, pp. 376-381

2016 Google
pp. 176-177

後藤武浩 Takehiro Goto
pp. 208-209

与田弘志 Hiroshi Yoda
pp. 210-213, p. 214 top, p. 215

Imprint, Architecture for Dogs
pp. 218-219 top row right/middle row
left/bottom row

Louis Bastian
p. 219 middle row right

木村三晴 Miharu Kimura
pp. 220-223

kenpo
pp. 232-235

尾鷲陽介 Yosuke Owashi
pp. 236-237, pp. 240-245, pp. 304-305

Felix Wey
pp. 270-271

Doug Meikle Dreaming Track Images /
Getty Images
pp. 302-303

Maider Lopez
pp. 320-321

志鎌康平 Shikima Kohei
pp. 324-325

後藤晃人 Akito Goto
pp. 328-329

Sebastian Mayer
pp. 342-343 background, p. 344
foreground, p. 350 left

Santi Caleca
p. 354 top, p. 356

繁田 諭 Satoshi Shigeta
p. 354 bottom, p. 355, p. 357

石巻工房 ISHINOMAKI LABORATORY
pp. 360-361, pp. 364-365, pp. 384-385

Nigel Bertram and Marika Neustupny
p. 369

金沢21世紀美術館 21st Century
Museum of Contemporary Art, Kanazawa
pp. 382-383
（撮影：木奥惠三 photographer: Keizo Kioku）

トラフ建築設計事務所 TORAFU ARCHITECTS
pp. 34-35, p. 46, pp. 50-51,
pp. 62-65, pp. 76-77, p. 80, pp. 96-98,
pp. 112-113, pp. 148-150, pp. 162-163,
pp. 186-187, pp. 252-253, p. 257
below, p. 268, p. 276, pp. 326-327,
p. 343 foreground, pp. 344-345
background, pp. 358-359

モデル Model
横尾光子 Mitsuko Yokoo
pp. 82-83

出典 Image Source
『ブイヨンの日々。』東京糸井重里事務所
Bouillon no Hibi (Days of Bouillon),
Tokyo Itoi Shigesato Office
p. 214 bottom

トラフ建築設計事務所 インサイド・アウト

2016年10月14日 初版第1刷発行

著者：トラフ建築設計事務所

発行者：加藤 徹
発行所：TOTO出版（TOTO株式会社）
　　　　〒107-0062 東京都港区南青山1-24-3 TOTO乃木坂ビル2F
［営業］TEL: 03-3402-7138　FAX: 03-3402-7187
［編集］TEL: 03-3497-1010
URL: http://www.toto.co.jp/publishing/

デザイン：中村至男
印刷・製本：株式会社 サンニチ印刷

落丁本・乱丁本はお取り替えいたします。
本書の全部又は一部に対するコピー・スキャン・デジタル化等の無断複製行為は、著作権法上での例外を除き禁じます。
本書を代行業者等の第三者に依頼してスキャンやデジタル化することは、
たとえ個人や家庭内での利用であっても著作権上認められておりません。
定価はカバーに表示してあります。

Ⓒ2016 TORAFU ARCHITECTS　Printed in Japan
ISBN978-4-88706-362-4

TORAFU ARCHITECTS: Inside Out
First published in Japan on October 14, 2016
Author: TORAFU ARCHITECTS
Publisher: Toru Kato
TOTO Publishing（TOTO LTD.）
TOTO Nogizaka Bldg., 2F 1-24-3 Minami-Aoyama, Minato-ku Tokyo 107-0062, Japan
[Sales] Telephone: +81-3-3402-7138　Facsimile: +81-3-3402-7187
[Editorial] Telephone: +81-3-3497-1010　URL: http://www.toto.co.jp/publishing/
Book Designer: Norio Nakamura
Printer: Sannichi Printing Co., Ltd.

Except as permitted under copyright law, this book may not be reproduced, in whole or in part,
in any form or by any means, including photocopying, scanning, digitizing,
or otherwise, without prior permission. Scanning or digitizing this book through a third party,
even for personal or home use, is also strictly prohibited. The list price is indicated on the cover.

ISBN978-4-88706-362-4